SPIRITS
AND
LIQUEURS

Andrew Durkan

TEACH YOURSELF BOOKS

ACKNOWLEDGEMENTS

The author would like to acknowledge and express his particular appreciation and thanks to all those who have been involved in the production of this book. He would especially like to thank those who answered his calls for specific information – their knowledge and assistance, so readily given, was invaluable. He is also very grateful to the following for their welcome guidance:

    Gilbeys of Ireland and many other liqueur elaborations
    The Irish Distillers Group Ltd
    The Scotch Whisky Association
    United Distillers Plc
    The Welsh Whisky Company Ltd
    John Cousins and colleagues at Thames Valley University.

Additional thanks and a debt of gratitude to June Dormer, Heinz Jaron, Philomena Leonard and Henry Wensley.

Long-renowned as the authoritative source for self-guided learning – with more than 30 million copies sold worldwide – the *Teach Yourself* series includes over 200 titles in the fields of languages, crafts, hobbies, sports, and other leisure activities.

Library of Congress Catalog Card Number: 96-72385.

First published in UK in 1997 by Hodder Headline Plc, 338 Euston Road, London NW1 3BH

A catalogue entry for this title is available from the British Library.

First published in US 1997 by NTC Publishing Group/An imprint of NTC Contemporary Publishing Company, 4255 West Touhy Avenue, Lincolnwood (Chicago) Illinois 60646 – 19975 U.S.A.

The 'Teach Yourself' name and logo are registered trade marks of Hodder & Stoughton Ltd in the UK.

Typeset by Transet Limited, Coventry, England.
Printed in England by Cox & Wyman Ltd, Reading, Berkshire.

Impression number	10	9	8	7	6	5	4	3	2	1
Year		2000	1999	1998	1997					

CONTENTS

FOREWORD

Welcome to the world of spirits and liqueurs. If you are interested in knowing about what you are drinking, this book is intended to help you. Globally the drinks world is changing and each generation seems to want to distance themselves from the drinking habits of their elders. People today want to drink less but to sample more, so there has been a significant broadening of people's tastes. Modern drinking trends veer towards favourite white spirits such as vodka and tequila and the consumption of luscious cream liqueurs. These are enjoyed alongside the more traditional favourites whisky, brandy, dark rums and gin. This broader trend has supported the introduction of 'alcopops', the new range of alcoholic fruit drinks, lemonades and colas. These remove the natural taste barriers that often deter people from drinking alcohol and may encourage people still drinking minerals to try them. By April 1997, alcopops had become the fastest-growing new alcoholic product of all time. The concern, of course, is that alcopops could habituate people to alcohol in childhood or early adolescence.

The drinks industry has a rigorous code of conduct in relation to drink promotion and advertising. The Advertising Standards Authority has drawn up strict codes of practice specifying four key areas that those responsible for drinks advertising should avoid.

1 Advertising should not be aimed at young people or specifically imply that drinking is a particularly macho or adult habit.
2 Advertising must not suggest or imply that drinking alcohol will make people more attractive or improve their performance in any way.

3 Advertising should not encourage excess either in the individual or the group or promote the concept of buying large rounds of drinks.

4 Advertising should not show any association between drinking alcohol and driving.

It is gratifying to note the moderation exercised by the general public in the consumption of alcoholic beverages in recent years. Leaders of the drinks industry also prefer to see an increase in the number of people who enjoy a drink, rather than to see individuals drink more.

The author hopes that this book will prove valuable as a general reference about spirits and liqueurs and that it will help consumers to increase their knowledge and their enjoyment of the product brands they purchase.

How to use this book

First there is an introduction to spirits and liqueurs. This includes the historical background to distilled and flavoured spirits. The principles of distillation and how alcoholic strength is calculated are explained. Some advice on healthy drinking is also given.

This is followed by a detailed examination of the various spirits and liqueurs. Spirits are mainly grouped according to type – grain spirits, fruit spirits, cane, vegetable and flavoured spirits. Liqueurs have their own separate section. Examples of classical mixed drinks are given throughout and there is a section on 'mixing them at home' which will help you to create all these wonderful drinks without fuss or bother in your own home.

A section on the culinary use of spirits and liqueurs follows, and finally some frequently asked questions are answered.

A comprehensive glossary of terms is provided at the end of the book, followed by a detailed index.

1
INTRODUCTION TO
SPIRITS AND LIQUEURS

Spirits are obtained by distilling fermented liquids. **Liqueurs** are spirits that have been flavoured, sweetened and sometimes coloured. The earliest distillations were made, not to produce alcohol but rather to make medicines, perfumes and elixirs. Greek and Egyptian alchemists started experimenting with distillates for pharmaceutical and culinary purposes. It is thought that the Arab physicians learned about distillation from the Greeks. By the tenth century they were producing a crude spirit called *El-Kuhl* from which the word 'alcohol' derived. The Arabs also fashioned for us words such as alembic (a type of still used for distillation) and elixir. Indeed the word distillation is, itself, attributed to Albukassen, an Arabian alchemist of the tenth century.

In the Middle Ages spirits were known in Italy as *aqua vitae*, in France *eau de vie* and in Celtic Ireland as *uisge beatha* – all meaning 'water of life'. In the eleventh century Italian distillers were making brandy from wine. By the twelfth century the Irish were distilling whiskey from beer and at about the same time the Poles and the Russians were making a flavourless spirit which they called *Zhizenennia Voda* – water of life – later to be known as vodka. Brandies were distilled in France in the fourteenth century and a century later Scottish Highlanders were distilling *uisge baugh* (whisky). In the sixteenth century, some time after the Italian Christopher Columbus introduced the sugar cane to the Caribbean, rum began to be made in the West Indies. In Normandy, France, a new apple spirit, Calvados, was produced about the same time. A medicinal spirit, later to be called gin, was produced in Holland in the seventeenth century. Rum, the first spirit to be distilled in America was made in the seventeenth century from imported West

Indian molasses. The eighteenth century saw the development of whiskey distilling in America. In the nineteenth century tequila emerged in Mexico as a distillate of 'mezcal wine'.

Liqueurs started to be made in an attempt to mollify the crude, harsh flavours of some spirits. Syrups were added to smooth the rough edges. Later, special herbs known to have medicinal properties were introduced. Spirits had long been used as antiseptics for dressing wounds and for healing sores, and when roots, plants and herbs were added – by infusion – to the spirit the new medicine became a universal remedy for most diseases. The great majority of these healing liqueurs were the results of experiments that were carried out in the monasteries of Italy and France. Monasteries in the Middle Ages were not only centres of learning, they were centres of healing as well. The monks grew their herbs and plants in their monastery gardens and infused them in alcohol to make their specialist remedies. Soon other flavouring elements – oranges, lemons, flower petals and honey – were introduced and that is how most of the ancient liqueurs evolved. The word 'liqueur' comes from the Latin *liquefacere*, referring to the method used in dissolving or melting flavours in a spirit liquid. The earliest documented liqueurs that we know of were bénédictine, first produced in 1510, amaretto in 1525 and kümmel in 1575.

Principles of distillation

Distillation is the extraction of alcohol from fermented liquids. It is based on three important factors.

- Ethyl alcohol vaporises when it reaches a temperature of 78°C (172°F) while water boils at 100°C (212°F).
- Water has a propensity to evaporate even at normal temperatures, so every distillation will include some water as well as alcohol.
- Minor constituents also known as congeners, which give a spirit its distinctive character of aroma and flavour, are also obtained in the vaporising process or by extractions from the residue. These constituents include fusel oils (higher alcohols other than ethanol), aldehydes, ethers, esters, volatile acids and organic compounds. These can be further enhanced as the spirit matures in wooden casks or barrels. Aldehydes which result from a combination of alcohol, acids and air are particularly important for the character

of a spirit. Esters are the volatile compounds formed by the combination of alcohol and acids, and these contribute to the bouquet or aroma of a spirit.

The art of distillation, therefore, is the selection and management of appropriate stills to heat the fermented liquids, and convenient condensers for collecting and liquefying the vapours. The two stills in general use are the pot still and the continuous or patent still – although there are also variations of these.

The pot still

This so called because it resembles an ancient cooking pot. The **pot still** looks like a giant onion and is made of copper which is a good conductor of heat. Copper also builds up a resistance to the effects of acids formed during the distilling process and which normally have the capability of dissolving metal. The design of the pot still is based on the alchemists' ancient alembic. It consists of a bulbous kettle in which the fermented liquid, known as 'wash', boils. On top of the still is a curved copper pipe called a swan's neck because of its shape. This leads the alcoholic vapours, boiled off during distillation, into a spiral tube or condensing worm made of copper coils. The worm is surrounded by cold, running water and as the vapours cool within the coils they liquify and fall as alcohol into a collecting vessel.

The pot still method retains the essential character of the basic ingredients. Each batch of fermented liquid is distilled twice, sometimes three times, to enhance the purity, quality and strength of the spirit. Because of its separate, low-temperature, slow distillations, the end product retains a good proportion of the congeners or flavour and aroma agents. That is why the pot still is always associated with the production of the big flavoursome spirits such as brandy, malt whisky, dark rum and the best quality Calvados.

The continuous still

This is also called the **patent still**. It is a complicated structure of two vertical columns, one called the analyser, the other the rectifier. Each column is sub-divided horizontally into chambers by perforated copper plates which have a drip pipe leading to the chamber underneath. Steam is injected at the bottom of the analyser and as it ascends the column it meets the wash that has already been heated in the rectifier. The steam strips the alcohol out of the wash and the vapours are carried over into the rectifier where they pass through a series of perforated plates. As the vapours rise they meet the cold wash being carried down the rectifier by the wash coil. This causes partial condensation which is completed when the vapours hit the cold water frame. By putting a non-perforated plate – known as a spirit plate – in the rectifier, fractions of any desired composition can be collected. The patent still has the commercial advantage of being reasonably cheap to operate. It can also deal with a continuous input of fermented liquid, producing spirits of very high strength and purity. In both the pot still and the patent still methods, each distillate is divided into three fractions – heads, hearts and tails. The heads and tails contain toxic compounds and other impurities and will be sent back for rectification (re-distilling). The heart which is the centre or best part of the distillation will eventually become the potable (safe for humans to drink) spirit.

Raw materials used in distillation

Any material that can be fermented can also be distilled. The basic wash (fermented liquid) used is based on three main ingredients – grain, fruit and vegetables. Some spirits such as gin and vodka can be made from either grain or vegetable.

Origins of the materials used for spirits and liqueurs

Spirits

Material	Drink
grapes (wine)	cognac, Armagnac and all other wine brandies
grain (beer)	whisky, kornbranntwein, vodka, gin (base)
sugar cane (molasses)	all rums, vodka and the spirit base for gin
dates, palm sap	arrack
blue agave (pulque)	tequila

Fruit brandies

apples	Calvados, applejack
plums	slivovitz, mirabelle, quetsch
cherries	kirsch
pears	eau de vie de poire
strawberries	eau de vie de fraise
raspberries	eau de vie de framboise

Compounded flavoured spirits

grain, molasses	gin
grain, potatoes	aquavit
grapes	pastis – Pernod, Ricard, ouzo
aromatic fruits	bitters
fruit, grain, grapes	liqueurs

Alcoholic strength

The early distillers had a unique and entertaining method of determining the alcoholic strength of spirits. They would mix equal quantities of spirit and gunpowder and then apply a flame to it. When the mixture failed to ignite it was considered too weak; if it exploded or burned too brightly it was too strong, but if it burned evenly and had a mild blue flame it was 'proved' suitable and safe for humans to drink. Hence the word 'proof'.

This primitive method lasted until late in the seventeenth century when a Mr Clarke invented a weighted float. When the float was dropped into a spirit it sank to a certain depth and this indicated the density of the liquor. From that knowledge the alcoholic strength could be calculated. Clarke was then able to calibrate a particular strength as 'proof'. Any liquor with a greater or lesser concentration of alcohol was 'overproof' or 'underproof' respectively.

Then along came Bartholomew Sykes (Sikes) who worked for the Board of Excise. He introduced his now famous Sykes hydrometer in 1816 and this was adopted by the Exchequer under the Hydrometer Act of 1818. Sykes, in his wisdom, determined that 100° was 'proof' and that pure alcohol was 175° or 75° overproof. So according to this scale, the figure for pure alcohol is 1¾ times the figure accorded to 'proof'. Alternatively, a spirit of 100° proof will contain 57.1 per cent alcohol and 42.9 per cent water. The Sykes system was adapted throughout the United Kingdom where spirits were sold at 70° proof (30° underproof). To convert the UK proof into percentage by volume all that was necessary was to multiply the proof by 100 and divide by 175.

$$\frac{70 \times 100}{175} = 40\%$$

If you think the British system complicated and hard to understand, the European system is logic itself – 0° is the absence of alcohol and

100° is pure alcohol – thus degree and percentage mean exactly the same. The system was invented by a French chemist Joseph Gay-Lussac (1778–1850) and was adopted throughout mainland Europe.

A third system was introduced in the United States whereby pure alcohol is reckoned as 200° proof, which means that proof is an exact balance of alcohol and water. Halving the 'proof' gives the percentage of alcohol by volume.

The British have now abandoned the abstruse system introduced by Sykes. The new system known as OIML (Organisation Internationale de Metrologie Légale) expresses alcoholic strength as a percentage by volume of alcohol. It is very similar to the Gay-Lussac system except that OIML measures strength at 20°C (68°F) and Gay-Lussac does so at 15°C (59°F), which gives a minutely higher reading. The difference is almost negligible except when deciding excise duty on large quantities of drink.

Approximate strengths of drinks

Drink	Alcohol by volume
alcohol-free	not more than 0.05%
de-alcoholised	not more than 0.5%
low alcohol	not more than 1.2%
reduced alcohol	not more than 5.5%
cider	4–6%, but specials go up to 8–10%
beer	3–6%, some go up to 8–10%
light wines (table wines)	8–15%, more usually 10–13%
Champagne and sparkling wines	10–13%
fortified or liqueur wines such as sherry and port	16–22%
aromatised wines such as vermouth	14–22%
vins doux naturels such as Muscat de Beaumes-de-Venise	15–18%
spirits such as brandy, rum, whisky	40%, some 45%
white spirits such as vodka	37.5% upwards
liqueurs	17–55%

Healthy drinking

Alcohol when taken in sensible amounts can be both pleasurable and beneficial. In fact, recent research has shown that light drinkers can lead healthier lives than those who don't drink at all.

Benefits of alcohol

Taken in moderation alcohol is a relaxant; it can also be considered a food as it generates heat and is a source of nutriment and energy. As an ingredient in a variety of drinks it can encourage social inter- course, sharpen the palate, accompany food, enhance flavours and help digestion. It is sometimes prescribed medicinally to help combat a variety of illnesses. Red wine is good for the heart, whisky can relieve the symptoms of the common cold and lower blood pressure, and gin is particularly useful in treating some kidney complaints and for flushing out the system. Brandy also offers some protection to the heart and blood vessels by raising the level of HDh cholesterol (the form of cholesterol that clears hard arteries). Sensible drinking can also accentuate sensory perception, sharpen the memory, depress cen- tres of anxiety and relieve tension and stress.

What are sensible amounts of alcohol?

The recommended safe drinking levels in Britain are 14 to 21 units of alcohol per week for women and 21 to 28 units per week for men.

A unit equals one of the following:

- ½ pint (284 ml) of ordinary beer or lager
- one glass of wine (125 ml)
- one glass of sherry or other fortified wine (50 ml or ⅓ gill)
- one glass of vermouth or other apéritifs (50 ml or ⅓ gill)
- one measure of spirits (25 ml or ⅙ gill)

A gill measure holds ¼ pint (142 ml) or 5 fluid ounces. The unit consumption should be spread over the week with at least one drink- free day.

Don't forget that in Ireland and Scotland spirit measures are more generous – equivalent to 1½ units and 1¼ units respectively. Remember also that extra-strength beers and lagers are far stronger than ordinary beers, and some low-calorie drinks contain more alcohol than their ordi- nary equivalents. It is estimated that more than 8.5 million of British people regularly drink in excess of the recommended levels.

What happens when you drink alcohol?

Most alcohol consumed passes into the bloodstream and is quickly absorbed. Sparkling wines including Champagne get into the bloodstream fastest of all. Food slows down the absorption of alcohol in the body, but the concentration of alcohol will depend on the height, weight, age and sex of the person. If you are small and slight of frame or if you are very young or very old you will be more easily affected by alcohol. Women also are more prone to the effects of alcohol because whereas men's body weight is made up of 55 to 65 per cent water, women have only 45 to 55 per cent water content. This means that alcohol, which is dispersed through the body fluids, becomes more diluted, less concentrated in men than in women. Almost all of the intake of alcohol is burnt up by the liver. What remains is discharged by urine or perspiration. But the liver can burn up only one unit of alcohol per hour, so if it is overtaxed over a number of years the liver will certainly suffer damage.

Short-term effects of alcohol

The effects will vary between individuals and whether or not they are drinking on an empty stomach. The following chart shows the reasonably typical effects of alcohol on a man of average build.

Number of units consumed	Effect on the person
1–2	Cheery, relaxed, confident.
2–3	More confident, which can also increase the risk of accidents.
3–4	Getting slightly merry, judgement may become impaired.
5	Above the legal limit for driving in the United Kingdom.
5–10	Depending on the nature of the person may be happy and very friendly or self-opinionated and argumentative.
10–12	Losing control – becoming maudlin or nasty or aggressive.
12–17	Becoming a nuisance, slurring speech, staggering, maybe even truculent.
18	Nearing toxic levels. Continued drinking will lead to unconsciousness.

Long-term effects of alcohol

Long-term heavy drinking can lead to serious illnesses such as liver cirrhosis, hepatitis, emotional disorders including depression, brain damage, high blood pressure, and can create even more problems for people suffering from diabetes. Heavy drinking will also impede the speed and quality of performance at work and may lead to dangerous or fatal accidents when people are driving or operating machinery. Continued heavy drinking makes people alcohol-reliant and those who become addicted may undergo personality changes and become extremely unpleasant and unreliable. Very often they will be unfit for work and become an embarrassment and a general burden to their families and friends.

Drinking and driving

The vast majority of serious accidents on the road are caused by drink/driving. People over the limit should not drive as their judgement will be impaired. The UK legal limit for car drivers is 80 mg of alcohol in 100 ml of blood. The number of units that takes you to the limit varies but for some it can be as few as three units.

How to get over a hangover

A hangover is the result of excessive consumption of alcohol. It gives you a thumping headache and can make you feel nauseous and absolutely wretched. Because alcohol is a diuretic and dehydrates the body, the brain cells also go through a physical change. As alcohol becomes absorbed water moves out of the body cells and the brain cells go through a withdrawal process, giving you a sore head. The headache will last until the brain cells again get accustomed to functioning without alcohol. You only have to experience a bad hangover to appreciate fully the necessity for avoiding another one. The practical solution is not to drink alcohol but to drink alcohol-free lagers, beers and wines. However, if you are going out to a celebration or to a party or function, or if you are going to enjoy a relaxing evening with friends, these drinks may not appeal. Taking sensible precautions is the best way to help counter the effects of your alcohol intake. As always, prevention is better than cure.

Before you drink

Eat food, as food slows down the absorption of alcohol in the body and consequently less alcohol gets to the brain. If you can't manage a meal or don't want to, take a banana or a glass of milk or fruit juice, or two evening primrose capsules to line the stomach before you set out. Milk, fruit juice and water taken before, during and after a drinking session will lessen the effects, including the 'trembly' sensation of dehydration. You might also try milk thistle and dandelion, obtainable from health food shops, as this helps the liver to detoxify the blood.

While you are drinking

If possible don't mix your drinks. Choose your favourite style of drink and stick to it. The saying that grape and grain do not mix is true, so avoid mixing beer and wine, and whisky and brandy. Red wine seems to bring on headaches for many people, but organic red wine is trouble free. Pot-still product spirits such as brandy and whisky are high in congeners (flavour agents) and may also contain traces of the toxic higher alcohols which can irritate the stomach lining. Opt instead for the purer spirits such as vodka which are congener-free. If you are using mixers, fruit juice is best of all as it accelerates the expulsion of alcohol from the body.

When you get home

Drink plenty of water to delay dehydration and take Alka-Seltzer or a similar remedy before going to bed.

The morning after

Most people have their own sure-cure remedy that they swear by for a hangover. So if you haven't bothered to take any evasive action and you are feeling at death's door you could try one of the following remedies.

Alka-Seltzer
This is good because it contains paracetamol and chemicals which counter the effects of alcohol.

'Hair of the dog'.
A dose of the same medicine does make you feel slightly better. However, the effect is only temporary which may tempt you to try another, and then another, and then you are back on track for another hangover.

Resolve
This 'cure' which you can get from a chemist, has many things to recommend it. It contains sodium bicarbonate which is a useful antacid and it helps to get rid of gas. It also contains glucose which gives you energy, and it replaces the vitamin C which alcohol has destroyed.

Big 'fry up'
If only you can hold it down, this provides energy and speeds the metabolism to flush out alcohol; but who can look at fried, greasy food when feeling so awful?

Prairie Oyster
This is a traditional favourite, made up of:

- 2 measures brandy
- 1 egg yolk
- 1 teaspoon wine vinegar
- 1 dash Tabasco sauce
- 1 pinch cayenne pepper

(The raw egg yolk puts some people off this one.)

Stir all the ingredients gently in a glass without breaking the egg yolk. Take a deep breath, and drink in one swallow. The shock, as much as anything else, will clear your head.

Herbal tea
Helps combat dehydration and speeds up the flushing out of the system. It also cleans the palate, but that's about all.

Bloody Mary
This concoction of vodka, tomato juice and Worcestershire sauce will do you no harm, but it is really only another excuse for a drink.

Underberg
Many regard this German brandy-based, herb-flavoured bitters as an infallible hangover cure. It is sold in single-nip portions and taken in one quick gulp.

'Hangover Over'
First take a paracetamol tablet and chase it down with fruit juice blended with a banana and honey. The paracetamol will soothe your sore head, the banana and honey will provide the glucose that will energise you, and the fructose will hasten the departure of alcohol from your body.

2
WHISKY

The word 'whisky' is synonymous with Scotland. Yet, fine whisky is also made in many other countries. In fact, the spirit originated in Ireland in the twelfth century when monks were distilling the stuff in their monasteries, for medical purposes of course. It is believed that Irish monks brought their whisky-making skills to Scotland in the fifteenth century. In turn, the Scots and the Irish introduced whisky distilling to the United States early in the eighteenth century. Today whisky is made also in Canada, New Zealand, Japan, India, the Czech Republic, Slovenia, Spain, Turkey, Brazil, South Africa, Australia and Wales. In Ireland and the United States whisky is spelt with an 'e'. All other countries leave out the 'e'. In its infancy whisky used to be known by the Gaelic name *uisge beatha* – meaning 'water of life'. The English found the name too long and unpronounceable so they latched on to the first word of the expression which they pronounced 'whisky'. The name stuck.

Making malt whisky

Whisky is a spirit obtained by distilling a fermented mash of cereal grains which have been saccharified – turned into sugar – by the diastase of malt. Each country has its own refinements in making the product, but the basic method revolves around using a pot still for making malt and heavy whiskies and using a patent or continuous still for making light-flavoured grain whiskies.

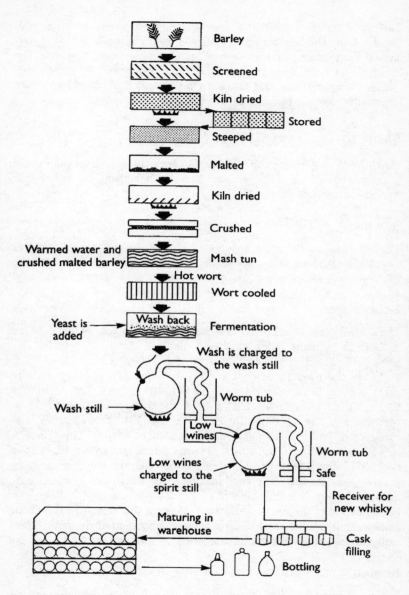

The pot still method

Barley is the essential and only grain used when making malt whisky. Only the finest quality barley is used and nowadays it is purchased from many sources including, of course, local farmers. The barley must be ripe, plump and dry, and free from any extraneous matter. It is screened and cleaned free of dust and other impurities before it is taken to be malted.

Malting

Malting is the germination of barley so that the starch in each grain is converted into a simple sugar. Malting has three distinct steps: steeping, germination and kilning.

Steeping

The barley is steeped or soaked in water in large tanks known as barley steeps. The soaking lasts for two to three days, during which time the grain absorbs water and oxygen, which encourages germination.

Germination

The soaked grain is drained and spread to an even depth of about 30 cm (1 foot) on malting floors which are made of stone or concrete. The barley is kept warm at a temperature of 16 °C (60 °F) and also moist, and over the next 12 days it is turned frequently, either manually using shovels or forks or by using mechanical devices. The reason for turning is to prevent the barley from sticking or matting together. Modern malting is done in a Saladin box – named after the Frenchman who invented it in the nineteenth century. This consists of a large revolving drum which is temperature controlled; this closer control of temperature and humidity speeds up the germinating process considerably. The combination of moisture and heat encourages the barley to germinate and each grain sprouts tiny rootlets. The barley secretes the enzyme diastase, making the starch in the grain soluble and capable of producing sugars, mainly maltose, for conversion, through fermentation, into alcohol.

Kilning

When germination has reached its peak further development is stopped by drying the barley, now known as 'green malt', in a kiln.

The grain is spread out on a perforated steel floor, which is heated and dried from underneath by a peat furnace or by smokeless anthracite or by air/fire fuelled by oil. When peat (known as 'turf' in Ireland) is used it can impart a rich peaty aroma and smoky taste to the final whisky. The special fragrance is known as 'peat reek' in Scotland. It is important that the kilning temperatures do not destroy the enzymes which have developed during germination, so the kiln temperature is kept below 70 °C (158 °F). Now follows the traditional stages of grinding, mashing, fermenting, distilling and maturing.

Grinding

When kilning is completed the ears of the grain have become chalky and soft, and the dried rootlets or malt combings are screened in dressing machines and removed to be sold for cattle fodder. The grain is ground in machines with steel rollers, and the usually rough ground grain is known as grist.

Mashing

The grist is put into a huge vat called a mash tun, and hot water is added. The quality of the water, which may have a peat, granite and heather influence, will have a most definite effect on the quality of the whisky. Some distilleries have their own springs, lochs and wells. Others draw water from streams and rivers. The water will have a starting temperature of 60 to 68 °C (140 to 155 °F) and the grist/water combination is thoroughly roused and agitated by revolving paddles. This action dissolves the sugars and produces a semi-transparant, non-alcoholic liquid known as wort. The wort is cooled through a heat exchanger to a temperature of 22 to 24°C (71 to 75 °F) and transferred to large vats known as washbacks. The remaining spent barley – known as draff – is sold later as cattle food.

Fermentation

The washbacks are traditionally large wooden containers made of pine or larch, but are now also made of stainless steel. These are three-quarters filled with the cooled wort, and then specially selected fresh yeast is added. Fermentation lasts for two days with the yeast converting the dextrose emanating from the maltose into alcohol and carbon dioxide. The result is a low-strength beer called wash. It is a beer in every sense except it lacks the flavour of hops. It will have an alcoholic strength of 5 to 10 per cent.

Distilling

In each distillery there will be at least two burnished copper pot stills. One is called the wash still, the other is known as the spirit or 'low wines' still. The shape of the still can have a bearing on the eventual character of the whisky. Stills with short necks tend to produce whisky of great intensity of flavour. Stills with long or high necks produce lighter-flavoured whiskies. The stills are heated from below by oil or gas or coke, or from within by steam-heated coils.

The wash is pumped into the wash still, the larger of the two stills, which has mechanical scrapers called rummagers. These prevent solid matter sticking to the bottom and imparting a burnt taste. Gradually the wash is brought to the boil. When the temperature of the wash reaches 78 °C (172 °F) the alcohol vapours rise into the neck of the still – known as a swan's neck because of its shape – and then through a condensing coil called a worm. The worm is a coiled pipe encased in a cold water jacket and it is here that the vapours are condensed into a distillate of low alcohol strength (about 30 per cent vol) known as low wines. The low wines now pass into the smaller spirit still where a second distillation takes place producing raw whisky. This colourless liquid is run into a glass-fronted spirit safe.

The still-man has now to make some vital decisions. He or she relies on experience and judgement when separating the distillate into three parts. The first part to emerge is known as foreshots which is pungent and impure. This is directed back to the low wine charger to be redistilled. The still-man will know when the foreshots have finished by a simple test. He will take a sample of the liquid and add a little water to it. If the liquid turns milky or cloudy the distillate is still foreshots. But if it stays clear the foreshots will have finished. The second part of the distillate is called the middle cut. This is the part that will be retained as raw whisky and be sent to mature. It will have a alcoholic strength of between 64 and 74 per cent by volume. The third part, known as aftershots or feints, produces weak, low-quality spirit which the still-man again directs to the low-wine charger for redistillation.

Maturing

The middle cut or heart of the distillation is put into storage vats where water of the same quality as was used in the mashing process is now added to reduce the alcohol content to 63.5 per cent alcohol (111° proof). This is considered to be an ideal maturing strength. The young, colourless whisky is put into oak casks of varying sizes where it will mature for a minimum of three years. However, most malt whiskies are cask matured on average for 8 to 15 years. The Customs and Excise inspectors allow for an annual 2 per cent loss through evaporation. This is known as the angels' share.

Casks

Casks impart flavour, texture and a distinctive aroma to whisky. Traditionally, the finest quality oak casks are used for maturing malt whisky. The size of the cask and the quality of wood is of great significance. Oak is favoured because it allows the spirit to mellow by breathing or taking in air. At the same time some of the more pungent and volatile alcohols can escape through the pores of the wood. But the quality of wood can vary depending on where it originated, whether it came from Europe or North America, and how it has been matured and whether or not it has already been impregnated. Many distillers use old sherry casks or rum casks, or a combination of these. Some distillers also use charred oak casks which have been previously used for maturing American bourbon whiskey, and it is interesting to see the distinct colour difference and, to a lesser extent, taste difference and flavour nuances that result from this practice.

Maturation is also influenced by the location of the cellar or warehouse. Warehouses by the coast and near rivers tend to facilitate a steadier rate of development than those sited inland. Whiskies matured in moist cellars lose less in volume than those with a hotter, drier storage temperature. The size of the cask will also have some bearing on how quickly the spirit will reach maturity. The larger the cask, the longer the whisky will take to mature.

Maturing casks are made in the following sizes:

- butt   108 gallons or 491 litres
- hogshead   55 gallons or 250 litres
- American barrel   38–42 gallons or 173–191 litres
- quarter   28 gallons or 127 litres
- octave   14 gallons or 63.5 litres

Smaller casks help to hasten maturation because more of the liquid is in contact with the wood.

There is, of course, a danger that prolonged ageing in cask will impart an undesirable woody taste to the whisky.

Grain whisky

Grain whisky gets its name because other grain, besides some malted barley, is used in the product. The main grain used is maize or wheat and this is ground into a fine flour. The flour is cooked in a steam-pressure cooker and the particles swell and burst to release their starch. A small amount of malted barley is added, and the malt enzyme diastase will convert the starch into sugar once the ingredients are mixed with hot water in the mash tun. The resulting hot wort is cooled and pumped into large containers called washbacks, where yeast is added. After fermenting for two days the wash is ready to be distilled.

Grain whisky is distilled not in pot stills but in a patent or continuous still which was perfected and patented by Aeneas Coffey, an Irish excise officer, in 1831. The still has two interconnected, copper-lined, vertical columns, one called the analyser, the other the rectifier. Each column is sub-divided horizontally by a number of perforated plates. Both columns are preheated by steam and the cool wash is pumped into the top of the rectifier where it descends down the column by way of a long, serpent-like pipe or coil. The heated wash passes out of the rectifier and is taken into the top of the analyser. The wash is freed from the coil pipes and as it descends the column it is met by a current of raw steam which has been introduced into the bottom of the analyser.

The steam strips the wash of its alcohol, and as the alcoholic vapours rise they are led by a pipe into the bottom of the rectifier. The spent or used wash is removed from the bottom of the analyser. Meanwhile the alcoholic vapours and steam start to rise in the rectifier. They meet at certain points the cold wash which is being carried down by the wash coil in the rectifier. This causes partial condensation, with the vapours getting cooler and the wash, on its way to the analyser, getting warmer. When the vapours reach the top of the rectifier they are condensed on a cold radiator or water frame before being drawn off as alcohol. The foreshots and feints – the first and last part of the

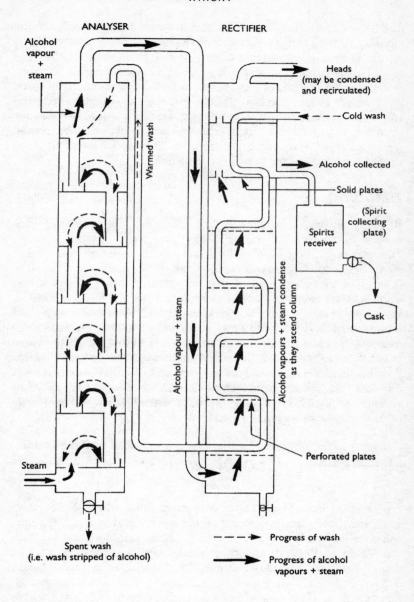

Coffey or patent still

distillate – are full of impurities and are sent to be redistilled. The middle cut, the potable fraction, is very pure but not completely so. It retains some congenerics and has an alcohol strength of about 95 per cent. This is reduced by water to a maturing strength of 69 per cent. It is put into oak casks where it must remain for a minimum of three years before it can be called whisky. Because it is light in body the spirit will mature much faster. Grain whisky destined for de-luxe blends or to be sold as a single grain self-whisky will mature in cask for many years. However, most grain whiskies go for blending when the three-year maturing period is completed.

Blending

Blending may be done using only malt whiskies but **blended whiskies** are associated with the mixing of malt and grain whiskies together. The more malt in the blend – the proportion is usually between 20 and 50 per cent – the more expensive the product. The main aim of blending is to get a consistent product that will please those who buy it and drink it. Most blenders blend to a formula. Once the blend is decided, the selected casks are taken to the blending hall. Here they are emptied into a trough and the spirit flows into a huge blending vat, where the contents are roused and agitated. After thorough integration the blend is run into casks and left to 'marry' for between one and six months. Blending is an art and a blender may use up to 40 different whiskies of different flavours and ages and which may have come from different regions and distilleries. If an age appears on the bottle it will be the age of the youngest whisky in the blend.

——————— Scotch whisky ———————

Scotch was little heard of publicly until 1664 when the Scottish Parliament attempted to tax it to finance the Royalist army. The outcome led inevitably to evasion, illicit distilling and to insobriety. With the Union of England and Scotland in 1707 an excise board was established, but their taxes on malt in 1713 and an increased tax in 1725 only led to rioting and an increase in illicit stills. Almost all farmers in the Highlands of Scotland had their own stills and the production of whisky for private consumption was regarded as a natural part of the farming cycle. When the English finally defeated the Scots at the Battle of Culloden in 1746 they made the Highlands accessible, by building new roads and bridges, to the Lowlands, and Scotch became accessible to everyone. The English also sent in their tax men to extort what were considered unfair duties on the spirit and, of course, the licensed distillers in the Highlands rebelled and continued to distill in secret, deep in the glens and other inaccessible locations.

From 1757 to 1760 due to crop-failure distilling was prohibited and farmers with private stills took the opportunity to gain access to a thirsty English market, although they were not legally allowed to sell their whiskies. They got over this by smuggling the stuff, and their cunning to outwit the 'gaugers', their name for the customs men, was inspired. One ruse was to stage funerals with the coffins concealing bottles of the fiery liquid. In the 1760s there was ten times more whisky made in private stills than in licensed stills.

In the 1770s the legitimate distillers lost patience and got together to petition Parliament, and in 1781 Parliament outlawed the private production of spirits. There was immediate uproar because by now the private producers considered they had an inherent right to distill. They also had the support of the great majority of the people who had been weaned on and preferred the contraband stuff. The private distillers resisted the ban with cunning and ingenuity and the situation became so chaotic that in 1823 there were 14,000 illegal stills uncovered. In the same year the Duke of Gordon, a landowner with immense power in Scotland, made a deal with the government. He said that if the taxes were equably adjusted and licensing made rational he and his influential friends would do their utmost to stop illegal distilling. The distraught government agreed and formulated the Excise Act of 1823. This reduced the duty on whisky to 2/3d per proof gallon and made licensing more realistic. Some people immediately took out licences to distill. They were not popular and incurred the wrath of almost everybody.

Gradually more enlightened and professional people came into the business and illicit distilling started to disappear. The more ambitious distillers began to spread their wings and gradually absorbed small firms. But there was only one thing wrong – newcomers to whisky drinking found the taste too strong. Then in 1827 Robert Stein, who distilled whisky in the Scottish Lowlands, developed a still which was later to be perfected and patented in 1831 by Aeneas

Coffey, a former Inspector General of Excise in Dublin. This new still, called the patent or Coffey still, produced a much lighter, almost bland whisky and it facilitated the use of other grain besides barley. These whiskies became popular especially abroad and were mostly used as a base for mixed drinks and cordials (liqueurs).

Early in the 1860s Andrew Usher started to blend these light-grain whiskies with the heavier, traditional malt styles. This resulted in a whisky with a lighter, smoother flavour but with a most definite whisky taste. It was destined to appeal to an international public and it was, and is to this day, the basis for the phenomenal success of Scotch whisky. When phylloxera, the dreadful vine disease which devastated most world vineyards, came to Cognac in the 1870s the making of brandy ceased. That left a gap and the Distillers Company Limited, formed in 1877 and aided by enterprising Scottish salesmen, ensured that Scotch would fill the vacuum. The Distillers Company was formed by six grain-whisky companies in and around Edinburgh. It had to defend its reputation and its product once when in 1905, due to the objections of malt distillers, a bill was passed forbidding the patent-still product from being called 'whisky'. The Distillers Company and others contested this in 1909. A Royal Commission reported as follows 'that the name whisky should *not be* restricted to the product of the pot still and that Scotch is a spirit obtained by distillation from a mash of cereal grains saccharified by the diastase of malt and distilled in Scotland'.

Today, more than 90 per cent of all malt whisky made goes for blending with the patent-still product, giving us such world-famous brands as Johnnie Walker Black Label, Bell's, Chivas Regal, Famous Grouse and Teachers, to name but five. But, of course, Scotland still makes her renowned pure malt whiskies which are revered through-out the world. The Scots claim that three natural influences make their malts so outstanding.

- **Water**, which comes from the hills to the stills, is of the greatest purity, filtered through rock and granite in the Highlands and though the chalk base of the Lowlands. In the making of malt, water is important for steeping, mashing and for the reduction of strength for maturing and bottling.
- **Purity of the air** is the reason why so many distilleries are sited away from pollution-prone locations. This is very important because while the whiskies are maturing in cask they are breathing in the air that surrounds them.

- **Wood used for casks** Oak is used as it allows the spirit to breathe and mellow. The Scots do not use new oak casks, they use casks that have already been seasoned by other liquors such as sherry or bourbon. These casks impart a flavour nuance and also contribute towards colour.

Types of malt produced in Scotland

Single malt is the product of one single distillery. Whiskies of varying strength and ages are mixed together to ensure a consistent product. The whisky can be sold after three years of maturing but usually it is kept in cask between 8 and 15 years before being bottled. The age that appears on the bottle is that of the youngest whisky in the bottle.

Single cask malts have been produced from one single distillation and when matured are bottled straight from the cask. They are not blended with any other whiskies produced in the distillery. They are the finest that a distillery can produce and are very expensive but are considered to be worth the price.

Vatted malts are produced mainly by big companies. Single malts of varying ages are usually bought in from different distilleries and are blended together. Should a year appear on the label it will be that of the youngest whisky in the blend.

Famous malt-producing regions of Scotland

These are the Highlands and its sub-division Speyside, the Lowlands, Campbeltown and Islay and the Islands.

The Highlands

Highland malts are produced north of the line drawn from Greenock to Dundee. They can be light and delicate or medium or full bodied depending on where they are produced. They can also be nutty, spicy, herby, leathery and smokey, or phenolic (medicinal having the smell of seaweed, TCP or iodine).

Major brands

Aberfeldy	Balblair	Ben Nevis
Blair Athol	Clynelish	The Dalmore
Dalwhinnie	Deanston	The Edradour

Glencadam   Glen Deveron   Glen Garioch
Glengoyne   Glenlochy   Glenmorangie
Glen Ord   The Glenturret   Inchmurrin
Lochside   Millburn   North Port
Oban   Old Fettercairn   Pulteney
Royal Brackla Royal Lochnagar   Teaninich
Tomatin   Tullibardine

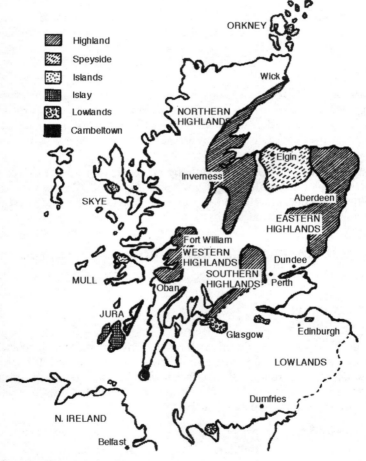

Malt whisky producing regions of Scotland

Speyside

This Highland sub-division is concentrated around the Elgin and Dufftown district. Most of the really classic malts are produced in this distillery-concentrated area. A great variety of styles are produced ensuring that there is a brand to suit every taste. The whiskies generally are big, distinctive, sweet and malty with lingering flavours. But there are also light, delicate more subtle styles too.

Major brands

Aberlour	An Cnoc	Ardmore
Aultmore	Balmenach	The Balvenie
Benriach	Benrinnes	Benromach
Caperdonich	Cardhu	Coleburn
Convalmore	Cragganmore	Craigellachie
Dailuaine	Dufftown	Glenburgie
Glendronach	Glendullan	Glenfarclas
Glenfiddich	Glenglassaugh	Glen Grant
Glen Keith	The Glenlivet	Glenlossie
Glen Moray	The Glen Rothes	Glentauchers
Imperial	Inchgower	Knockando
Linkwood	Longmorn	The Macallan
Miltonduff	Mortlach	Pittyvaich
The Singleton of Auchroisk	Speyburn	Strathisla
Tamdhu	Tamnavulin	Tomintoul
Tormore		

The Lowlands

Located south of the Greenoch/Dundee line: Glasgow and Edinburgh are within this region. The malts are soft, light bodied and somewhat gentle in character. They are perhaps the ideal introduction into malt whisky drinking. Because of their unassertive character they are often used for blending.

Major brands

Auchentoshan	Bladnoch	Glenkinchie
Inverleven	Littlemill	Rosebank
St Magdalene		

Campbeltown

This was once the capital of whisky distilling in Scotland. Now only two distilleries remain. These full-bodied whiskies are very distinctive, having a peaty, almost medicinal aroma with spicy, salty yet mellow-flavoured overtones.

Major brands

Longrow	Springbank

Islay

(Omit the 'y' for correct pronunciation.) These strong-flavoured and strong-smelling malts are distinguished by their intense peaty and smoky characteristics. Newcomers to whisky drinking may find their flavours overpowering but amongst seasoned malt whisky drinkers these whiskies have enormous prestige.

Major brands

Ardbeg	Bowmore	Bruichladdich
Bunnahabhain	Caol Ila	Lagavulin
Laphroaig	Port Ellen	

The Islands

Isle of Jura
This light smooth and subtle whisky has a refreshing, clean finish on the palate.

Brand: Isle of Jura

Isle of Mull
These are softly winning whiskies, very gentle and easy on the palate.

Major brands

Ledaig	Tobermory

Orkney
These clean, silky whiskies have a faithful following amongst serious whisky drinkers. They have a lingering pleasant flavour.

Major brands

Highland Park	Scapa

Isle of Skye
Produces a big, heavy, peaty, rich-flavoured malt.

Brand: Talisker

Twenty best-selling malts

Glenfiddich	Glen Grant	Glen Morangie
The Glenlivet	Glenfarclas	Macallan
Laphroaig	Aberlour	Cardhu
Glenkinchie	Highland Park	Knockando
Springbank	The Singleton of Auchroisk	Bowmore
Lagavulin	Isle of Jura	Talisker
Longrow	Bunnahabhain	The Tormore

Blended whiskies of Scotland

The blending of malt and grain whiskies started in real earnest in Scotland towards the latter part of the nineteenth century. The lightly flavoured grain whiskies were used to dilute the big, heavy malt-flavoured whiskies which were not generally popular in the international market. These 'new-style' whiskies became immediately popular. Before long they secured the fame and reputation of Scotch whisky throughout the world. Blending has become so sophisticated that the blenders' skills can produce consistent qualities, using different ratios of malt and grain, depending on the style required for a particular market. About 85 per cent of Scotch is now sold overseas.

Blended Scotch is made in three styles – standard, premium and de-luxe.

- **Standard Scotch** has the lowest malt content – about 20 to 30 per cent malt whisky in the blend.
- **Premium** has up to 45 per cent malt whisky in the blend.
- **De-luxe** has 50 per cent and over of malt whisky in the blend.

Twenty best-selling blended whiskies

Johnnie Walker Red Label	Bell's	J & B Rare

Famous Grouse	Ballantine's	Chivas Regal
Teachers	Grant's	Cutty Sark
White Horse	Stewarts Cream of the Barley	Haig
Black & White	William Lawson's	Whyte & Mackay
Vat 69	Clan Campbell	Claymore
Dewar's	Long John	

Distinguished de-luxe blends

Islay Mist	Scotia Royale	Pinwinnie
Old Parr	Johnnie Walker Black Label	Dimple
Chivas Regal	Big "T"	The Antiquary
Red Hackle	Usher's	Laird O'Cockpen
King of Scots	House of Lords	

——— Irish whiskey ———

It is generally accepted that the Irish were first to make whiskey. From an abundance of grain they fermented a beer wash which, with the aid of turf fires, they distilled into a crude spirit called *uisge beatha* – 'water of life'. Probably ancient traders from the Mediterranean, or St Patrick himself, brought the art of distillation to Ireland. Soldiers serving Henry II in his campaign in Ireland were introduced to the spirit in 1171, and it became a popular part of the booty to be taken home to England.

In 1608 Bushmills in County Antrim became the first distillery in the world to get a licence to distill whiskey. By 1770 there were more than 1,000 registered distilleries operating, but soon afterwards the law was changed to militate against the smaller operators and to benefit larger units so that excise supervision could become easier to administer.

By an Act of Parliament in 1823 distillers were encouraged to improve the product and to become more professional and efficient. As the industry became more streamlined new brands appeared and the home and export market grew. But then in the 1830s the Church-influenced temperance movement intervened and that, allied to the increasing popularity of beer, saw the sales of whiskey diminish. At the same time the Irish, who had been the prime producers of whiskey worldwide, lost the initiative to the Scots. In 1831 a new continuous still, ironically patented by Irish exciseman Aeneas Coffey, was introduced. This would enable distillers to make inexpensive grain whiskey more quickly and more economically. The product could then be blended with the traditional heavier malt whiskies, resulting in a lighter, smoother and more international-friendly spirit. The Irish were reluctant to court the new technology but the Scots were quick to embrace it and, allied to native commercial expertise, were soon dominating the market.

By 1885 there were only 28 distilleries operating in Ireland. The years of prohibition in the United States (1919–33) put an end to that market and the declaration of the Irish Free State in 1922 did likewise, for a time, to the English and British Empire markets. When things became reconciled new generations of whiskey drinkers had developed a preference for other whiskies – principally for Scotch.

In 1966 the Irish whiskey industry, now down to five companies, was rationalised. Tullamore Dew, John Jameson & Son, John Power and Son and the Cork Distillers Company, which included Paddy, came together to form the Irish Distillers Company. Bushmills joined the group in 1972. With the exception of Bushmills, which remains on the banks of the Bush river in County Antrim, all the other brands are produced in a huge modern high-tec distillation complex in Middleton, Co. Cork. The distillery has the facility to produce the precise individual styles of whiskey which have been evolved over a century by each individual company. So each brand looks, smells and tastes exactly the same as the original product did. The amalgamation has been a great success and Irish whiskey is once again popular on world markets, as it deserves to be.

The Irish Distillers Company is now owned by the French giant Pernod/Ricard and Tullamore Dew was bought by UK's Allied Distillers in 1993. However, a new independent Irish-owned distillery called Cooley was launched in Dundalk in 1987. It produces both malt and blended whiskies which are gaining steadily in popularity. Although pure malts have been made by Bushmills since 1985 and Cooley since 1992, the main business is in blended whiskies, most of which have a high proportion of malt in the blend. This is exemplified by the renowned Bushmills Black Bush whose malt content is 80 per cent of the total. In Ireland the malted grain is normally dried in closed kilns and not over turf fires. So the peaty, smoky flavour traditional with Scotch is deliberately absent. Irish premium brands are triple distilled in pot stills to impart a smoother texture. They are oak aged for a minimum of three years. In practice however, they are kept in cask for between 5 and 15 years. Patent-still products, when used, are also well matured and when mixed with the blend add a lightness and gentleness to the already smooth malt.

Well-known brands

Bushmills 1608
Bushmills Black Bush
Bushmills Single Malt
Coleraine
Cooley (Tyrconnel Malt, Kilbeggan and Locke's Blended Whiskies)
Jameson (Ireland's best seller on the world market)
Paddy (also known as Paddy Flaherty)
Power's Gold Label
Tullamore Dew

Middleton Very Rare

This distinctive, brilliant and very costly whiskey was first launched in 1984. It is Ireland's most expensive whiskey but it is worth the price to experience its smooth, silky taste. It is super-premium whiskey made in limited batches and vintage bottled.

American whiskey

The Irish and the Scots brought their distilling skills with them to America. The first whiskies were made in Pennsylvania, Maryland and Virginia without any legal interference from the Government. In 1791, soon after George Washington became President, the Government, desperate for money, decided to levy an excise tax on whiskey. This led to a three-year whiskey rebellion which saw people rioting and the tax collectors being given a rough time – some were even tarred and feathered. Feelings and resentment were so high that Washington had to send in his troops to quell the rebellion. Fortunately, this was accomplished without bloodshed.

The disillusioned farmer-distillers moved out, travelling down the Ohio river and into Kentucky out of range of the revenue men. Here they found fertile land for the growing of grain and, most importantly, the ideal water that has been purified coming through layers and layers of limestone rock. Rye was the main grain crop used for whiskey making, until one year when the rye crop partly failed. Then corn was added to the rye mash and the resulting distillation had a much improved flavour and character. Whiskey became a prosperous business and during the 19th century played an important part in the opening up of the West. Whiskey became the popular drink in the boom-town saloons, refreshing the miners and the cowboys and inflaming the redskins whenever they got a hand on it.

In the East the industrial settlement started to expand, and then continued growing with the influx of thirsty immigrants from Europe. This provided opportunity for widening the whiskey market. In 1911 more than 370 million litres of whiskey were produced. The booming sales of hard liquor outraged the sober minded who campaigned militantly against it on the premise that alcohol consumption would eventually lead to self-abusement and, in turn, threaten the quality of family life. The suppression of the manufacture, sale and consumption of all alcoholic drinks resulted and was ratified by congress when they passed the Volstead Prohibition Act in October 1919. This deprivation lasted until 20 February 1933 when the Act was amended and subsequently ratified in December, just in time for Christmas celebrations. Prohibition lead to wholesale flouting of the law, and during these 13 'dry years' only bootleggers, if they survived, could tell the real story.

How American whiskey is made

The principal grains used are maize (corn), rye, millet and barley. The grain is cleaned and coarsely ground into a meal. Heated limestone-water is added and the combination is thoroughly roused, the sugars are dissolved and the liquid becomes wort. The wort is cooled ready for fermenting. Two yeasting processes are widely used in America – the sweet mash process and the sour mash process.

In the **sweet mash process**, fresh yeast is added to the mash and fermentation takes place resulting in an alcoholic liquid known as distillers' beer.

The **sour mash process** uses the residue or fresh hot slop from a previous distillation. This is added to the mash, together with some fresh yeast. Sour mash gets its name from the fact that the weak spent beer left over in the stills is fairly acidic. However, the resultant whiskey after distillation is certainly not sour. The sour mash process contributes towards the continuity and character of a particular whiskey brand.

Distillation

The distillers' 'beer' or wash is taken to a patent or continuous still and after distillation will have an alcoholic strength of 160° US proof (80 per cent by volume). This is diluted using limestone-water to 103° US proof (51.5 per cent alcohol) and sent to mature in charred oak casks. The charring of casks was first used as a method of cleansing the inside of the casks. Certainly the burnt insides contribute towards colour and aroma and mellowness.

Styles of American whiskey

Straight whiskey is usually made from one type of grain, for example rye or corn. If subsidiary grains are added the main grain must dominate and be at least 51 per cent of the total volume. These full-bodied whiskies are matured for at least two years in charred oak casks. Blended straight whiskey is a blend of two or more straight whiskies.

Blended whiskey must contain at least 20 per cent of straight whiskey in the blend. This will be stretched with additions of neutral spirit and other whiskey styles, such as light whiskey. Neutral spirit is sometimes referred to as 'silent spirit'. It is distilled to 190° US proof (95 per cent alcohol volume). Distilled to this strength the spirit virtually loses all its flavour. When added to the blend, the whiskey becomes lighter and less flavoursome. Nevertheless, it is a very popular style and accounts for about 25 per cent of the domestic market.

Light whiskey was introduced on 1 July 1972. It is distilled at 160° US proof (80 per cent alcohol volume) and is stored in used or uncharred, new oak casks before being bottled at 40 per cent of alcohol. The whiskey lacks real character as the flavour is very slight.

Corn whiskey is made from a mash containing 80 per cent corn (maize). It gets little ageing and has a raw, robust, fiery flavour.

Rye whiskey is one of America's finest styles. It is made from a mash containing at least 51 per cent rye. It may be classified in three ways: straight, blended straight or blended. These whiskies are mostly associated with Pennsylvania and Maryland. The whiskies are traditionally full-bodied and rich in aroma and flavour.

Bottled in bond whiskies. Only straight whiskies are bottled in bond. These whiskies are the product of one distiller and are bottled at 100° US proof (50 per cent alcohol) and stored in government warehouses for a least four years or until the distiller wants to withdraw them. At this point the distiller pays the appropriate tax to the Internal Revenue. The green stamp over the stopper authenticates the 'bottled in bond' guarantee, but the term does not have any special quality status.

Main categories of American whiskey

Bourbon

Bourbon was first made in Bourbon Country, Kentucky, hence the name. The Reverend Elijah Craig, a Baptist minister, is credited with being the father of bourbon whiskey. In 1789 he set up a still beside a limestone creek in Georgetown, Bourbon County. He used maize (corn) as the main grain, principally because it was more abundant than other grains, and called his new whiskey Bourbon County Whiskey. The use of charred oak barrels is also attributed to Craig. Apparently he was heating some white oak staves to make them pliable for bending into barrels. Something distracted him and on his return he found some staves had been heavily scorched. He made these into a barrel and discovered later that the whiskey in this particular barrel was far superior to any in the batch. He experimented further and found that the charring process allowed the whiskey to soak into the wood, giving softer, more mellow and toasted overtones to the spirit. Bourbon is made from at least 51 per cent maize (corn) mainly using the sour mash process. It is matured in new, charred oak barrels for a minimum of two years. If left overlong maturing in barrel the new wood will impart a pronounced oaky aroma and flavour.

Major brands

Ancient Age	Early Times	Elijah Craig
Four Roses	I. W. Harper	Heaven Hill

Jim Beam (world's best-selling bourbon)	Kentucky Tavern	Maker's Mark
Old Charter	Old Crow	Old Fitzgerald
Old Forester	Old Weller	James E. Pepper
Rebel Yell	Wild Turkey (big seller in America)	Evan Williams

Tennessee

Tennessee whiskey is straight whiskey distilled in Tennessee from a mash that contains a minimum of 51 per cent corn. Its production is somewhat similar to that of bourbon, except that a unique filtering system is used to help to produce the smooth, rich flavour associated with the Tennessee style. Slats of sugar maple are burned and hosed with water. The resulting charcoal is packed into 10 foot-high (3 metre) vats and the raw spirit is slowly filtered through the charcoal. Sometimes virgin wool blankets are placed underneath and on top of the charcoal. This diffuses the spirit on the way through and gives a more uniform filtering system. The spirit takes ten days to pass through the charcoal in the vat. Often the whiskey is twice charcoal-filtered – once before and once after maturation – which contributes to the traditional mellow, smoky flavour.

The whiskies are aged in charred, white oak barrels for four to six years and take on a smooth, mellow character. Most is produced by the sour mash system. Only two whiskey distilleries operate in Tennessee: Jack Daniels, first established in Lynchburg in 1866, and George Dickel, built in Cascade Hollow, Tullahoma in 1879. Both distilleries produce a variety of excellent brands, but Jack Daniels sells better on the international markets. Its premium brand, Gentleman Jack, is a delight and the company motto 'Each day we make it, we'll make it the best we can' says it all.

Canadian whisky

Whisky distilling began in Canada late in the eighteenth century. The original location was Kingston on Lake Ontario and from here whisky-making spread along the St Lawrence and Great Lakes districts where grain farming was a prime occupation. In 1875 the Government decreed that Canadian whisky must be made of cereal products using

the continuous still method of distillation and that a three-year maturation in cask was to be a basic minimum requirement.

Canadian whisky, light and bright, quickly gained approval, and during
the American Civil War and later during Prohibition the Americans
developed a taste for it. In Canada's own Prohibition period, it was customary in restaurants to serve the whisky from silver teapots with milk
jugs in matching design holding water or another preference. Winston
Churchill on a subsequent visit to Canada insisted that his whisky be
served in like fashion.

Canadian whisky is made from a mixture of grains – rye, barley, corn
and wheat. The quality of the spirit depends on the following factors:

- The mix and proportion of the grains used.
- The quality of the water.
- The special strains of yeasts used for fermentation.
- The variations that result when different column lengths are used
  in the continuous or patent still. The taller the column the lighter
  the whisky that emerges.
- The casks used for maturing the spirit. They may be new and
  made of charred oak or they may have been previously used and
  impregnated with sherry or brandy or bourbon. Each will impart a
  certain flavour and colour character to the spirit.
- The length of time the spirit matures in cask will also have a bearing
  on quality as each constituent whisky in any blend will have an
  optimum maturing age. Canadian whisky is usually matured six
  years or more before it is released for sale.
- The conditions of storage, heat, moisture and the quality of air in
  the warehouse will have an influence.
- Canadian whisky is entirely based on blending. Up to 20 whiskies
  distilled at strengths varying from 140° to 180° proof may be used.
  The proportion of each used in the blending formula is the
  distiller's secret, but most blends will have a zesty, rye influence.

The traditional Canadian whisky is light-bodied, smooth, soft and delicate with a suggestion of sweetness.

Major brands

Black Velvet   Canadian Club
Canadian Mist   Crown Royal

Seagram's V. O.   Schenley's Golden Wedding
Corby's Royal Reserve   Wiser's De Luxe

Japanese whisky

Two men, Masataka Takatetsuru founder of Nikka and Shinjiro Torii founder of Suntory, are regarded as the fathers of Japanese whisky. Takatetsuru studied applied chemistry at Glasgow University and later worked in distilleries at Rothes and Campbeltown. He returned to Japan in 1920 where he joined Torii to establish a whisky plant, Suntory, in 1924. The first whiskies went on sale in 1929 and went into direct competition with the traditional schnapps-style spirit schochu. After World War 2 Japanese youth became influenced by the US lifestyle which included whisky drinking. The whisky the Americans drank was too expensive, so they turned to the tariff-free Suntory product. Tory bars were successfully established throughout the country and continue to flourish.

Takatetsuru left the Suntory Company in 1934 to establish his own distillery which he later renamed Nikka. He died in 1979 at the age of 85 and by that time his whiskies had established a 20 per cent hold on the Japanese market. In contrast, Suntory dominates the market with 70 per cent of the domestic sales. Both companies use the pot and continuous stills for their distillations and mature their whiskies in American white oak barrels, or in charred oak casks or in old sherry and bourbon casks. Each company makes pure malt whiskies as well as de-luxe blends and more mundane blends. Sometimes imported whisky may be used to enliven blends.

Brands of Japanese whisky

Major brands from Nikka

All Malt   Gold & Gold
Grand Age   Hi
Pure Malt Black   Pure Malt Red
Pure Malt White

Rye base
Super Nikka
The Blend Selection
Tsuru

Major brands from Suntory

Hibiki	Kakubin
OLD	Reserve
Royal	Suntory White
Yamazaki	

— Whiskies from other countries —

Notable brands

Australia	Corio
Brazil	Natu Nobilis
Czech Republic	King Barley
India	Bagpiper
	Maqintosh
	McDowells
	Men's Club
	White House
New Zealand	Lammer Law
	Wilsons
Slovenia	Jack & Jill
South Africa	Teals'
	Three Ships
Spain	DYC
Turkey	Ankara
Wales	Prince of Wales
	Swn y Mor

Drinking whisky

Whisky can be drunk on its own (neat), or with ice (on the rocks), or mixed with water (still or sparkling) or mixed with minerals such as lemonade or cola. Pure malt whiskies and their equivalents are usually taken neat. If you are a newcomer to whisky drinking you should try them in their natural state first, then, if they are too strong for your taste, add a dash of water which will gently alter the strength, adding a little more, in stages, until you settle on the level that suits you.

Whisky makes an excellent apéritif and a good aged malt is superb as a digestif. As a nightcap to ensure untroubled sleep, whisky reigns supreme.

Classic mixed drinks using whisky as a base

Manhattan

2 measures rye whiskey
1 measure sweet vermouth
1 dash Angostura bitters
ice

Stir all the ingredients together. Strain into a cocktail glass. Decorate with lemon peel and a cherry.

Mint Julep

2 measures bourbon whiskey
6 mint leaves
1 tablespoon caster sugar
soda water
crushed ice

Put the sugar and mint into a highball glass. Add a splash of soda water and thoroughly mash the mixture until the sugar is dissolved. Add the bourbon and fill the glass with crushed ice. Stir well until the outside of the glass becomes frosted. Decorate with mint and serve with two straws.

Klondike

2 measures Canadian whisky
2 measures apple brandy
1 teaspoon white crême de menthe
dash of grenadine
ice

Shake vigorously with ice. Strain into an old-fashioned glass, half-filled with crushed ice.

Whiskey Punch or Hot Whiskey

1 generous measure Irish whiskey
2 teaspoons golden brown sugar
1 thick slice of lemon (no seeds)
4 whole cloves
boiling water

Put the whiskey, sugar, and the lemon slice studded with cloves into a heat-proof glass. Pour boiling water on top. Stir to blend.

Old Fashioned

1 measure bourbon whiskey
1 teaspoon caster sugar
1 teaspoon water
2 dashes Angostura bitters
ice

Mix the sugar, water and bitters in a mixing glass. Add the whiskey and ice cubes. Stir and pour into a rocks glass. Decorate with a slice of orange and a maraschino cherry.

Flying Scotsman

2 measures of Scottish malt whisky
1 measure green chartreuse
1 teaspoon egg white
ice

Shake ingredients vigorously with ice and strain into a cocktail glass. Decorate with cherries.

Irish Cocktail

2 measures Irish whiskey
1 measure green crême de menthe
½ measure green chartreuse
ice

Place all the ingredients into a shaker. Shake vigorously. Strain into a cocktail glass. Decorate with a green olive and a cherry.

Grand Central Station

1 measure bourbon
1 measure light rum
1 measure brandy
2 teaspoons lemon juice
2 teaspoons caster sugar
ice

Shake all the ingredients together vigorously. Strain into a cocktail glass.

Kentucky Colonel

2 measures bourbon
½ measure Bénédictine
ice

Shake all the ingredients together well. Strain into a cocktail glass.

Yellow Knife

1 measure Canadian whisky
1 teaspoon yellow chartreuse
2 teaspoons orange juice
ice

Shake all the ingredients together vigorously. Strain into a cocktail glass.

Balmoral

1 measure Scotch whisky
1 measure gin
¼ measure anisette
ice

Shake all the ingredients together. Strain into a cocktail glass.

Bobby Burns

2 measures Scotch whisky
1 measure sweet vermouth
1 measure dry vermouth
dash Bénédictine
ice

Shake all the ingredients together. Strain into a cocktail glass.

White Shadow

1 measure whisky
1 measure Pernod
1 measure thick double cream
grated nutmeg
crushed ice

Put all the ingredients into a shaker. Shake well and strain into an old-fashioned glass. Sprinkle with grated nutmeg.

Niagara Falls

2 measures Canadian whisky
1 measure Irish Mist
1 measure thick double cream
grated nutmeg
ice

Shake all the ingredients vigorously. Strain into a cocktail glass. Sprinkle with grated nutmeg.

Louisburgh Lunch

1 measure Irish whiskey
1 measure Irish Mist
1 measure ginger wine
ice

Put all the ingredients into a mixing glass. Stir well with the ice and strain into a wine goblet.

Black and Tan

2 measures Irish whiskey
1 measure dark rum
½ measure lime juice
½ measure orange juice
¼ teaspoon caster sugar
ice cubes
chilled ginger ale

Put all the ingredients, except the ginger ale, into a shaker. Shake well. Strain into a tall glass and top up with ginger ale.

Rye Toddy

2 measures Rye whiskey
1 measure lemon juice
1 teaspoon caster sugar
1 thick lemon slice studded with 3 cloves
1 cinnamon stick
boiling water

Put the studded lemon slice into a mug. Add the whiskey, sugar and cinnamon stick. Pour in the boiling hot water and stir.

Whisky Sour

2 measures whisky
1 measure lemon juice
½ measure gomme syrup (i.e. sugar and water made into a syrup)
dash of egg white
ice

Shake all the ingredients together vigorously. Strain into a goblet.

Rattlesnake

2 measures whisky
½ measure Pernod
juice of a lemon
1 pinch icing sugar
1 teaspoon egg white
half zest of an orange
ice

Put all the ingredients into a shaker. Shake well with ice. Strain into a goblet.

Black Hawk

2 measures whisky
1 measure sloe gin
ice

Place all the ingredients in a mixing glass. Add ice. Stir well and strain into an old-fashioned glass.

Sand Dance

1½ measures whisky
1 measure cherry brandy
2 measures cranberry juice
ice

Fill a highball glass with ice. Pour in all the ingredients. Stir well.

Alcazar

1½ measures Canadian Club whisky
1 measure Bénédictine
dash zest of orange
cherry
broken ice

Half-fill a tumbler with broken ice. Add the ingredients. Stir well. Strain into a cocktail glass. Decorate with a cherry.

Cold Kiss

1½ measures whisky
½ measure peppermint schnapps
2 teaspoons crème de cacao
crushed ice

Shake all the ingredients vigorously with crushed ice. Strain into a cocktail glass.

Frisco

1½ measures whisky
½ measure brandy
½ measure lime juice
½ measure lemon juice
twist of lemon
ice

Shake all the ingredients well with ice cubes. Strain into a whisky sour glass. Decorate with a twist of lemon.

Golden Glow

1½ measures whisky
½ measure dark rum
¼ measure orange juice
¼ measure lemon juice
dash grenadine syrup
ice

Place the spirits and fruit juices in a shaker along with the ice cubes. Shake vigorously. Strain into a cocktail glass. Add a dash of grenadine syrup on top.

St Andrews Cocktail

1 measure Scotch whisky
1 measure Drambuie
1 measure orange juice
ice

Shake the ingredients well with ice. Strain into a cocktail glass.

Godfather

1½ measures whisky
¾ measure amaretto
ice

Pour the ingredients over ice cubes into a whisky glass. Stir gently.

Horse's Neck

1½ measures whisky
dry ginger ale
1 lemon
ice

Cut the rind from the lemon juice in one continuous spiral. Fill a highball glass with ice cubes. Add the whisky. Top up with ginger ale. Stir gently. Decorate with the lemon rind.

3
BRANDY

Brandy is the concentrated goodness of wine. Fundamentally, brandy is the distillation of wine. The name is derived from the Dutch term *Brandewijn* which means 'burnt wine', a reference to the heat applied to wine in a still. But the name brandy is also used to embrace distillates made from other fruits such as Calvados from apples, slivovitz from plums, kirsch from cherries. In France these are more correctly known as *eaux de vie de fruits* whereas brandy is referred to as *eau de vie de vin*. Grape brandy is made in all wine-producing countries; the products from France, Spain, Portugal, Italy, Germany, California, Australia, Israel, South Africa and South America all enjoy international reputations. Some countries make brandy for home consumption only.

Of all brandies the French, especially Cognac and Armagnac are the most highly regarded. The French laws of controlled appellation demand territorial integrity, as well as controlling the type of vines to be used and in what density these are planted. This in turn, determines yield and regulates quality. Distilling also obeys fixed regulations ensuring that spirits produced elsewhere will never be used to adulterate the native spirit. Cognac and Armagnac brandies have set standards of quality by which all other brandies are judged.

Cognac

The Cognac area was officially delimited by a French decree on 1 May 1909. Cognac lies inland from the Bay of Biscay and follows

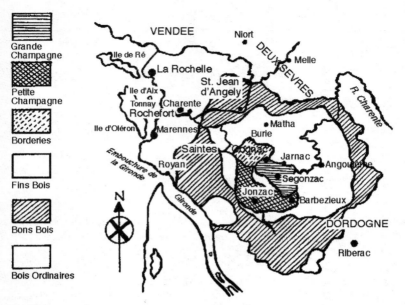

Grande Champagne

Petite Champagne

Borderies

Fins Bois

Bons Bois

Bois Ordinaires

The Cognac region

the meandering River Charente before it flows into the Atlantic near La Rochelle. The area is located in the *départements* of Charente and Charente Maritime in south-west France and is officially divided into six sectors or zones. These form concentric rings round the town of Cognac and are known by the following appellations.

1 **Grande Champagne** Located south of the towns of Cognac and Jarnac this innermost sector full of chalk and limestone produces fine, elegant and most delicately fragrant brandies. These classic brandies take 15 years or longer maturing in cask before they reveal their exceptional qualities. The word Champagne has nothing to do with the celebrated sparkling wine. Here it conveys the French interpretation indicating a region of chalky soil. The name comes from the Latin *campania* meaning field or cultivated area.

2 **Petite Champagne** This larger area is second only to Grande Champagne in terms of quality. There is a slightly smaller proportion of chalk in the soil which is less friable. This brandy ages more quickly and becomes mellow sooner, but it tends to be lighter in body.

3 **Borderies**   This small zone has only half the carbonate of lime found in the sectors already mentioned. The brandy made here ages rapidly and is more robust, lacking the delicacy and elegance associated with fine brandies, but it does give body to any blend.

4 **Fins Bois**   The soil here is looser and more pebbly. The brandies produced are sound rather than spectacular and they age rapidly. Bois means wood as the slopes of the hillsides were covered with trees before being cleared and turned into vineyards.

5 **Bons Bois**   This zone has a variation of richer soil, including clay and sand. The brandies are pleasant but a bit thin and sometimes have a earthy flavour (*goût de terroir*).

6 **Bois Ordinares/Bois Communs**   Due to the proximity of the Atlantic, the soil has now become more sandy. The salt winds give these thin brandies a distinctive earthy flavour. The use of sea-weed as a fertiliser may also influence the flavour. Major distillers rarely use any of the Bois grapes to make their classic styles.

The distillation of Cognac started somewhere between 1620 and 1630. Heavy taxation on wine at the time meant that only a small propor-tion of the wine was sold. This inevitably led to overproduction, so the farmers, in order to save space and preserve the wine, started to distill. In the late seventeenth century, Dutch and Scandinavian salt merchants who did their customary business through the port of La Rochelle had developed a taste for this coarse, crude wine.

Recognising that taxation was levied on bulk and not on alcohol strength they decided to boil down the wine – ostensibly for ease of transport – and called it *brandewijn* ('burnt wine'). They found, as many more were to find, that the new spirit tasted better than the old wine. Rich traders started to establish distilleries in the region. Some came from abroad, notably Jean Martell from Jersey in 1715 and Richard Hennessy from Ireland in 1765. As the distillations became more sophisticated the product became more appreciated. By 1830 Cognac was exported worldwide in barrel and in bottle.

The vines

Cognac is made from a combination of three white grape varieties – the Ugni Blanc, the Colombard and the Folle Blanche. The **Ugni Blanc** accounts for over 90 per cent of the total production and is known locally as St Emilion Charente. The grapes are thick skinned and sturdy and not prone to disease. The **Colombard** is sensitive to the oidium disease and requires frequent spraying with sulphur. This grape produces a harsh spirit. The **Folle Blanche** is thin skinned and is also prone to disease but the vine is a big yielder.

All Cognac vines were ravaged in 1876 by the dreadful disease known as phylloxera. Since that time all vines are grafted on to American root stock to keep them healthy and phylloxera free. The grapes when pressed make a thin, acid wine which is low in alcohol – 7 to 10 per cent by volume. As a table wine it is harsh and borders on the unpleasant. It is sometimes drunk locally as an accompaniment to shellfish. But the wine's greatest virtue is that it forms the perfect base for distilling into brandy. The high level of acidity in the wine lessens the chance of spoilage by microorganisms and the low level of alcohol dictates that a higher volume of wine is required, so that the flavouring compounds, through distillation, will become more concentrated and enriched. It is estimated that it takes ten bottles of wine to make one bottle of Cognac.

What makes Cognac so special?

- Nature of the **soil**, predominantly chalk and limestone with some intrusions of pebbles, clay and sand.
- **Climate**, which is influenced by the Atlantic and the Gulf Stream. The salty winds bring an abundance of rain in winter and spring and help to keep the vines healthy. Cognac has a temperate climate with an annual average temperature of 12 °C (54 °F).
- Specialisation of **vine selection** which has proved to be in harmony with soil and climate.
- **Viticulture** – the farming and care of the vineyards which promotes maximum quality standards.
- **Vinification** – the making of the wine which is left in its natural state, not racked or clarified or matured before distillation.
- **Distillation** – the wine is distilled in a pot still which retains the congenerics, the flavouring elements and aromatic compounds which give character and personality to a spirit.
- The **maturing process** – Cognac is aged in wood and only improves in wood. The type of wood used – Limousin oak – is special to Cognac, contributing to colour, tannin, aroma, flavour and mellowness. It also allows the spirit to oxidise and develop its bouquet.

- The **cellar** or **warehouse** – the conditions in the warehouse allow the spirit to mature gradually and without any hiatus in development.
- **Blending** – the art of the blender is crucial to the quality of the final brandy. Cognac blenders are renowned for their ability to produce the best possible product.

How Cognac is made

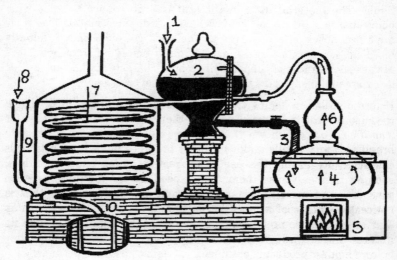

1.	Wine	5.	Heat source	9.	Cooling water
2.	Pre-heater	6.	Spirit vapour	10.	Brandy
3.	Heated wine	7.	Condenser coil		
4.	Copper pot	8.	Water source		

Cognac still

Although some major distillers own vineyards and make their own wine, most buy grapes or wine – even young Cognacs – from local farmers. After the grapes have been gathered and brought in from the vines they are pressed and the juice is fermented into a wine – albeit a harsh wine. It is said locally that the best Cognacs are made from the worst wine. That may be so, but the wine must be healthy and sound as any blemishes would be carried through the distillation and show up later.

The new, unaged wine is put into a still. The still used is a pot still, known in Cognac as the *alembic Charentais/Cognaçais*. The design of the still was perfected in the seventeenth century by the Dutch. The still consists of a huge copper kettle or boiler encased in a brick framework with provision for an open furnace underneath. On top of the boiler is a *chapiteau* or hood from which a pipe shaped like a swan's neck protrudes. This carries the vapours through or past a preheater and then into a condensor coil which is kept immersed in cold running water. It is here that the vapours are converted into a liquid. The material used in the still is pure copper because wine being distilled throws off acids which can dissolve metal. The acids have less effect on copper and as the stills get older they gradually build up a resistance to the acids. Spirits emerging from new stills always show traces of copper. This copper character is known as *goût de cuivré* and disappears after about a year of cask ageing.

Before distillation begins two important decisions have to be made: the size of still to be used and whether or not to use a preheater (*chauffe-vin*). It is known that smaller stills make more distinctive brandies. Larger stills make smoother brandies but with a little less character. Regarding the use of preheaters, some major distillers, such as Hennessy, use them. They speed up the distilling process, save fuel and most importantly, prevent the scalded taste that is noticeable when cool wine is put on to a hot surface. Others such as Martell do not use preheaters, as they feel that wine should take its natural course through the distilling process and by so doing, they believe a purer product is obtained.

In the making of Cognac, there are two separate distillations. The first is called the *premier chauffe*. The wine is taken from the fermenting vats, with or without its lees, and is put into the boiler. If the lees or impurities are added, some believe, they give a fuller character to the spirit. The heat source, slow and regular, brings the temperature to 78 °C when the alcohol vaporises. The vapours are taken by tube through the preheater (if used), thereby heating the new wine about to be distilled. From there the vapours are conducted into the condenser where they are converted into a liquid. The first liquid to emerge from the still is called *produit de tête* or 'heads'. It is pungent and contains ethers and is almost toxic and certainly unpleasant. It is removed and added to the new wine about to be distilled. The next liquid to emerge is technically known as the *brouillis* (boiling up), but in distilling terms it is also known as the heart or best or centre part of the distillation. It is put to one side and has an alcoholic strength of between 25 and 30 per cent by volume. The final liquid to emerge from the stills is known as *produit de queue* or 'tails'. This is very low in alcohol – the water is also vaporising by this time – and is full of impurities. It is added along with the heads to the new wine.

The still is then carefully cleaned, the new wine is added and the whole process is repeated twice more. It takes three lots of *brouillis* to fill the still for the second distillation, which is known as the *bonne chauffe* (the good heat). Whereas the first distillation takes about 10 hours, the second distillation will take 14 hours or more. The aim is to extract maximum alcohol and flavourings. Again there will be heads, hearts and tails. The heads and tails will be separated and added to the oncoming brouillis. The heart will be the new brandy, raw, white with harsh overtones often accentuated by copper. It will have a definite bouquet and an alcoholic strength of 70 to 72 per cent by volume. The new spirit is known locally as *la vigne en fleur* – 'the vine in flower'. The new colourless Cognac is put into new casks to mature.

Maturing of Cognac

Cognac is matured in casks made from Limousin oak. Limousin, east of Angoulême, has always been a natural forest. The wood, so important to Cognac, has the right degree of porosity and tannin content. Before being made into casks the wood is matured for seven years – four years in the open and three years under cover, but with access to air. This dries the wood and some soluble extracts evaporate. Sometimes young Cognacs are stored in wood which comes from the forests of Tronçais in central France. This wood is harder, less absorbing, and has less tannin than the Limousin quality. It is mostly used for short-term storage. Casks vary in capacity, but the ideal size of cask for maturation holds 350 litres (92.5 gallons).

The conditions of storage are also important. Many of the warehouses are located near the river which creates damp storage conditions. Brandies lose bulk in dry warehouses and lose strength in very damp warehouses, so a happy medium is sought. Young casks absorb a liberal quantity of spirit and the spirit absorbs tannin from the wood. Some tannin is necessary for mellowness and flavour but too much gives the spirit a woody flavour which is highly undesirable. So the young brandy is left for about six months before being transferred to older casks. During its time in cask, air will penetrate the pores of the wood and this causes the brandy to lose its harsh and fiery character. Oxidation, which also takes place through the porous wood, will develop bouquet and taste. Some tannin will be absorbed and some colour and flavour too, but while older casks will mellow the spirit they have less to offer in terms of character building as the wood has now become more neutral.

The rate of oxidation is relative to the humidity in the warehouse, but during the ageing process in cask – which can last in some cases up to 50 years or more – 2 to 3 per cent of alcohol escapes into the air annually. This is why the buildings around the warehouses have a black, sooty appearance. The loss through evaporation is known locally as the 'angels' share'. The distillers estimate that they lose the equivalent of 2 million bottles annually, but they are philosophical about it, merely saying 'the sun is our best customer'. To make up for the loss each cask is refreshed or topped-up annually with spirit of the same quality.

Blending

When Cognac is required for sale the skill of the blender comes into play. The blender has to marry together the contents of many casks, taking into account the length of time the spirit has matured and the special characteristics that individual casks have imparted to the spirit during storage. Sometimes wonderful and extraordinary old Cognacs are stored in a section of the warehouse called *le paradis*. The blender may decide to use some of this quality to give the blend an uplift. The main aim is to get a consistent product that is typical of the distillery's style and worthy of its name. Nearly all Cognacs will have to be diluted to a potable (safe for humans to drink) strength, usually 40 per cent by volume. This is done gradually over a few months by adding distilled water or *petites eaux* – a combination of weak brandy and water. Then the final touches are added – a little caramel to enhance the colour and a little sugar syrup to soften the blend. Cognac is filtered before being bottled to ensure a star-bright appearance. Once bottled it will remain constant. It will not mature any further.

Well-known brands

Bisquit
Courvoisier
Delamain
Hennessy
Martell
Polignac
Renault

Camus
Davidoff
Delon
Hine
Otard
Rémy Martin

Label terminology

Internationally Cognac may not be sold until it is at least three years old, and age always refers to the youngest brandy in the blend. Terminology is nearly always confusing because age indicators are not consistent from company to company. For example, a three-star Cognac could mean a three-year-old, cask-matured spirit for one company and a five-year-old product for another. However, below is a general guideline.

Three Star or **VS** (very special) suggests three to five years of cask maturation.

VSOP (very superior old pale or product), **VO** (very old) or **Réserve** are all known as fine quality or liqueur Cognacs. They are not sweet, but are finely matured having spent from 7 to 17 years in cask.

XO (extra old), **Grande Réserve**, **Extra Vielle**, **Hors d'Age** and **Extra** are old liqueur Cognacs; in other words brandies of great age and refinement – the very finest products of the Cognac houses. They will have matured in cask for 20, 30, 40 years or more.

Grande Fine Champagne is a brandy made exclusively from grapes grown in the Grande Champagne zone. It is the ultimate brandy, elegant in style and when aged to perfection has unrivalled finesse.

Fine Champagne is another excellent style of Cognac. It is made from grapes grown in the Grande Champagne and Petite Champagne zones and must have a minimum of 50 per cent Grande Champagne grapes in the blend.

Fine Maison is usually a quickly matured Cognac which is made specifically for a group of outlets or restaurants or for an individual restaurant that wishes to market the brandy under its own name and label – in other words BOB (a buyer's own brand). The product is usually smooth and delicate, offering good value.

Early-landed Cognac. It was fairly customary at one time, but not so much today, for some British merchants to ship quantities of young Cognac – a year or so old – to Britain so that it could mature more slowly in cask in the cooler, damper bonded warehouses in London, Bristol and Leith. This practice produced a brandy of great smoothness that was eventually sold under the importer's name. The label showed the date the spirit was shipped from Cognac and when it was bottled.

Armagnac

Armagnac is the other great French brandy. It was first distilled in the fifteenth century, so it even predates Cognac. Until the Dutch, trading from the port of Bayonne, discovered the attractions of *eau de vie d'Armagnac* the spirit had only a local reputation. Because of its inland location there had been great difficulty in getting the product to market, and, with the exception of the Dutch, this continued to be a commercial problem until the 1830s when the River Baise was made into a canal and linked to Bordeaux. Trade immediately developed, but by then Cognac had been firmly established as the world's favourite brandy.

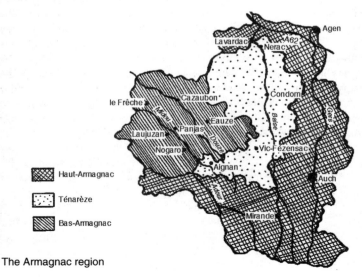

Haut-Armagnac

Ténarèze

Bas-Armagnac

The Armagnac region

Armagnac is produced in the Gers *département* in the heart of Gascony. The region was delimited in 1909 and divided into three zones of production: Bas-Armagnac, Ténarèze and Haut-Armagnac.

Bas-Armagnac is the source of the really outstanding Armagnacs. The soil is rich with a topsoil of *boulbène*, a fine alluvial deposit – a legacy of the time when all this part of south-west France was under water – covering a subsoil composed predominantly of sand and some clay. Eauze is the zone's capital and the brandies produced are full, rounded and supple with a bouquet of prunes and plums.

Ténarèse surrounds the capital Condom. The soil is a mixture of *boulbène*, chalk and clay, producing fast-maturing, full-flavoured brandies with a perceptible floral scent of violets.

Haut-Armagnac lies around the town of Auch, and is the largest of the three sectors. It has classic chalky soil and produces good table wines, but the poorest of all wine for making into brandy. Instead, when the wine is distilled the spirit is mainly used as a base for liqueurs or for preserving fruit – like the local speciality prunes in Armagnac.

Grapes

The speciality grapes are the Ugni Blanc (St Emilion), Picpoule (Folle Blanche), Colombard and the Hybrid Baco 22A. The latter is a cross between the Folle Blanche and the American grape Noah. It was introduced after the Armagnac vineyards were devastated by the aphid phylloxera in 1893. The hardy and reliable Ugni Blanc is the mainstay of production, accounting for four-fifths of the land under the vine. The Baco is disliked by Brussels because it is a hybrid and will be banned from the year 2010. Already the Baco is being phased out with the Ugni Blanc almost always taking its place.

Making Armagnac

Armagnac is made in a still unique to the region. The still was purposely developed in the nineteenth century and is a modification of the continuous still. It has, however, a much shorter condensing column, and therefore it can produce a spirit low in alcohol – about 53 per cent by volume – thereby retaining a good proportion of the organic

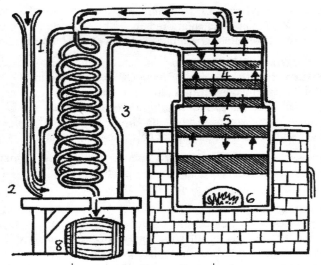

1. Wine	4. Baffled Column	7. Spirit Vapour
2. Pre-heater	5. Copper Pot	8. Brandy
3. Condenser	6. Heat Source	

Armagnac still

compounds, even impurities which give flavour, aroma and an earthy, rustic charm to the spirit. The stills are easily transportable and are moved about the district to service the needs of the small growers. Since 1972 the pot still has also been used to make Armagnac, and this type of still produces a mellower, stronger spirit.

Maturation

Armagnac in youth is absolutely colourless. It is put into dark-coloured casks made from the sappy Monlezun oak, which comes from the forests of Bas-Armagnac. This wood, which imparts colour to the spirit, is also noted for its fast-maturing qualities. The casks are never kept full to the brim as oxidation is considered beneficial to the maturing process. During maturation in the cool, dark cellars, the spirit loses some of its fire and earthiness. A good Armagnac should be round and smooth with no hint of harshness. But it will always retain a trace of pungency and a suggestion of fire.

Label terminology

Armagnac is sometimes cask matured for 20 years or more. However, as it ages faster than Cognac it usually gets less time to mature in wood.

Three stars indicates cask maturation of between one and three years.
VSOP indicates four years in cask.
VO, **Hors d'Age** indicate more than five years in cask.

Some houses offer vintage Armagnacs which are made from grapes grown in an outstanding year. They may also specialise in Bas-Armagnac blends which they are always keen to emphasise on labels.

Well-known brands

Baron de Sigognac
Château Garreau
Château de Malliac
Clés des Ducs
Domaine de L'Escoube
Janneau
Marquis de Caussade
Marquis de Puységur
Samalens

Chabot
Château de Laubade
Château du Tariquet
Domaine Broustet
Dupeyron
Larressingle
Marquis de Montesquiou
De Montal
Sempé

——— Other French brandies ———

Besides the big two – Cognac and Armagnac – other French brandies are made from selected lots of non-*appellation contrôlée* wines. These brandies are made essentially for the export market and are popular duty-free items. They are blended to a recipe and are matured in cask to an acceptable smoothness. Many of the companies are based in Bordeaux. Their aim is to produce a uniform product which offers good value to the customer.

Popular brands

Bardinet Napoléon
Beehive Premium Reserve

Grand Empereur (Rémy Martin owned)
Raynal Three Barrels

Cortel Premium
Domet Napoleon
Dorville

Ronsard
La Ruche Premium Reserve
De Valcourt

Fine

Fine is another style of French brandy made in many wine areas. It is distilled from poorer, rougher wines. Marc (pronounced *mar*) is another. It is made from the lees or pomace left over after the main pressing of the grapes has been completed. Some of these distillations are crude and fiery and have the effect of sending searchlights through your body. But there are exceptions and these better qualities will have been matured in cask for ten years or more. They are quite smooth and palatable. In France, it is customary to dip a sugar cube into the marc and then suck the spirit out.

Good brands

Marc d'Alsace (when made from
   Gewürztraminer grapes)
Marc de Bourgogne
Marc de Champagne
Fine de Bordeaux

Fine de Champagne
Marc de Condrieu (Rhône)
Marc d'Arbois (Jura)
Vieux Marc de Bandol
   (Provence)

Marc's equivalent is known as grappa (grape stalk) in Italy and California. It becomes Tresterbranntwein or Tresterschnapps in Germany, bagaçeira in Portugal, aguardiênte in Spain and dop-brandy in South Africa.

—— Brandies from other countries ——

Australia

There is a thriving brandy business in Australia. The main centres of production are in New South Wales, Victoria and South Australia. Both the pot still are continuous still are used. The new spirit is oak-aged and kept in cask from a minimum of 2 years to usually a maximum of 25 years.

Label terminology

Old means a minimum of 5 years cask age.
Very-old means a minimum of 10 years in cask.
VSOP means up to 25 years in cask.
Other styles such as **Seven Star XO** will have brandies aged from 20 to 50 years in the blend.

Well-known brands

Hardy's Black Bottle   Angove's St Agnes
Seppelt's Château Tanunda   Best's St Andrew's
Thumm's Château Yaldara   Penfold's Stock

Brazil

Seagram's make a good Brazilian five-star brandy called Macieira. It is cask-aged and mellow.

Cyprus

Brandy production started on this Mediterranean island in 1868. Both pot- and continuous-still products are made and the best styles are aged in Limousin oak.

Well-known brands

Haggipavluś Anglias   Sodapś Adonis
Keoś Five Kings   Peristiani V031

Czech Republic

Czech brandy is often a blend of pot-still and continuous-still products. It is usually aged in oak casks. A good example is **Seliko's Slovignac**.

Germany

German brandy is usually made from wine imported from France and Italy. These brandies are distilled mostly by the pot-still method.

Well-known brands

Asbach Uralt
Decker's Dupont and Steinalter
Eckes Chantre and the big selling Mariacron
Pabst & Richarz Pfalzer Weinbrand (made from German grapes)
Racke's Dujardin Imperial

Greece

Metaxa is the well-known brandy from Greece. It is double distilled in pot stills and is oak aged.

Israel

Brandy is made in Israel using the pot and continuous stills. The better styles have aged in Limousin oak casks. **Askalon's Grand 41**, **Carmel's Richon 777** and **Barkan's Stock 84** are popular brands.

Mexico

Mexico makes fine brandies after the Spanish style. The best qualities, like **Presidente** (the biggest selling brandy worldwide), are made by the pot-still method and matured and blended by the solera system.

Other popular brands

Almacenes Guajuardo   Martel
Casa Madero   Don Pedro

South Africa

Brandy is considered to be the the national drink in South Africa. It is made in most wine regions and the best styles are distilled and matured in the Cognac tradition.

Well-known brands

Backsberg	Mellow-Wood
Barrydale	Mons Ruber
Boplaas	Oude Meester
Clos Cabrière	Paarl Rock
Fine de Jourdan	Richelieu
Fish Eagle	Ryn
KWV	Viceroy

Spain

Brandy production in Spain is divided into two categories: *brandy de jerez* and *brandy del penedès*.

Brandy de Jerez

This is made by most sherry producers. When distilled the brandy is put through the solera system – the traditional way of blending and maturing sherries. This accelerates the maturing period and is known as 'dynamic ageing' elsewhere.

Well-known brands

Bobadilla 103

Luis Caballero	Conde de Garvey, also Espléndido
Cardenal Mendoza	González Byass Lepanto
Conde de Osborne	Valdespino
Domecq who makes Carlos I, Carlos	Williams & Humbert Gran
111 and the famous Fundador	Duque d'Alba
Duff Gordon	

Brandy del Penedès

These brandies are gaining a good reputation, especially those associated with the two foremost producers Mascaró and the ubiquitous Torres. Most brandies are made by the pot-still method and aged traditionally in Limousin oak. However, some are a blend of pot- and continuous-still products, and ageing and blending through the solera system is sometimes practised.

Special brands are:

Mascaró Estilo Fine Marivaux	Miguel Torres Imperial

Narciso Eqiqueta	Miguel 1
Don Narciso	Honorable

Italy

Italy makes many fine brandies using the pot-still and continuous-still method of distillation. Most are cask aged, often in Slovenian oak.

Popular brands

Branca (of Fernet Branca fame)	Oro Pilla
Carpenè Malvolti	Stock 84
Fogolâr	Vecchia Romagna
Inga XO	Villa Zarri

Of course, Italy is famous for another style of brandy called grappa. This brandy is made from the pomace – the skins, stalks, pips and debris left over in the wine presses. Water is added to the murky mass, then it is fermented and immediately distilled. Some of the best grappa is made by using pot stills.

Distinguished brands of grappa

Ceretto	Libarna
Con Senso	Lungarotti
Gratacul	Marolo
Inga	Nardini
Julia	Nonino
Romano Levi	Vite d'Oro

United States brandy

Most brandy distilled in the United States is made from Californian wine. The spirit has long been a tradition in California and before Prohibition (1919–33) it was a customary part of a wine-maker's general output. When the Prohibition Act was repealed, the distillers had to start from scratch, but by 1938 there was such a glut of table wine in California that brandy distillation was actively encouraged. This helped matters, as it allowed stocks to be built up and gave the opportunity for the brandy to be matured properly. Californian brandy is not like European brandy. It is lighter, has its own character regarding bouquet and taste; it must be judged on its own merits. The modern brandies are made from selected wines which have the characteristics most suitable for distilling. Both the pot and continuous stills are used and the new spirit is matured in American white oak or Limousin oak barrels for between 2 and 12 years. Sometimes old bourbon whiskey barrels are used in the maturing process, as they impart a deeper colour and a richer, fuller flavour to the product. The two most popular grapes for making the basic wine are Thompson's Seedless and Flame Tokay, but the classic Cognac grapes Ugni Blanc, Folle Blanche and Colombard are also used, as are the Muscat, Pinot Noir, Gamay, Palomino and Chenin Blanc.

Much of the popular 'mixing' brandy is made by the continuous-still method which produces a clean, very light brandy with a smooth finish. It is used as a base for cordials, cocktails or with mixers such as ginger ale or orange juice.

The 'sipping' brandies have more flavour and depth of body. These are made entirely by the pot-still method or sometimes from a blend of pot- and continuous-still products. When they are made by the double-distillation pot-still method the better-quality brandies are generally matured in Limousin oak barrels for a minimum of five years.

Well-known brands

Bonny Doon	Germain–Robin
Carneros Alembic	Jepsom
Christian Brothers	Korbel
Crown Regency	Paul Masson
Domaine Charbay	RMS (Rémy Martin owned)
E & J (from the Gallo winery)	

Grappa

American grappa or pomace brandy is made mostly in California, but some is also made in Oregon and other wine states. The pomace of many grape varieties is utilised, including Barbera, Cabernet Sauvignon, Zinfandel, Gewürztraminer, Muscat and Malvasia. Some producers also use whole grapes with or without the leftovers, and use small pot stills to extract maximum flavour and full perfume. The best producers use oak casks – often Limousin oak casks – for maturing their grappas. Others dispense with wood ageing altogether to preserve the natural freshness of the spirit.

Some well-known brands
Bonny Doon
Clear Creek (Portland, Oregon)
Creekside
St George Spirits

South America

Pisco is a brandy native to Peru and Chile. It was first made in the seventeenth century and takes its name from the Peruvian port Pisco from whence it was shipped. The Incas called it *pisku* meaning 'flying bird' – an apt description. The best-quality piscos are made from two grape varieties, Moscatel Rosado and Moscatel de Alejandria. The wine produced has an alcohol strength of about 13 per cent. This is put into a still modelled on the alembic Charentais, goes through a single distillation with heads and tails being eliminated and added to the oncoming wine. The centre or heart of the distillation will have an alcohol strength of about 55 per cent. This raw spirit was traditionally matured in porous clay jars and consumed quite young. It is more usual nowadays to put the young spirit into small casks made of oak or beech, where it will mature for 6 to 18 months. It is then diluted with distilled water and graded according to its final alcohol strength: **selección** 30 per cent, **Especial** 35 per cent, **Reservado** 40 per cent, **Gran Pisco** – which also gets the most ageing in wood – 43 per cent.

Pisco is white in colour and dry in flavour. You can drink it neat or with a mixer such as papaya juice. For some, the most satisfying way to drink the spirit is as Pisco Sour which can be bought ready made, but it is best to make it yourself.

Pisco Sour (for two)

2 measures of pisco brandy
4 measures of lime juice
2 teaspoons of caster sugar
1 dash of Angostura bitters
a very small amount of egg white
ice

Shake thoroughly with ice and strain into an old-fashioned glass. Decorate with sliced lime.

Drinking brandy

Brandy balloons are the best glasses to use when drinking brandy. They curve narrowly at the top to contain the aroma, and the glass is very thin which allows the spirit to be easily warmed by hand and so both bouquet and flavour are enhanced. Brandy is usually taken neat as a digestif, but it can also be combined with mixers such as soda water, ginger ale or lemonade. For these latter long drinks, only the cheaper varieties of the spirit should be used.

Classic mixed drinks using brandy as a base

Corpse Reviver

1 measure brandy
½ measure Calvados
½ measure sweet vermouth
ice

Stir with ice and strain into a cocktail glass. Add a twist of lemon.

Copacabana

1 measure brandy
1 measure apricot brandy
½ measure Cointreau
2 teaspoons lemon juice
ice

Shake with ice and strain into a cocktail glass. Decorate with slices of orange and lemon.

Sidecar

½ measure brandy
½ measure Cointreau
½ measure lemon juice
ice

Shake with ice and strain into a cocktail glass. Decorate with lemon peel.

Between the Sheets

½ measure brandy
½ measure white rum
½ measure Cointreau
1 dash lemon juice
ice

Shake with ice and strain into a cocktail glass. Decorate with a strawberry.

Dream Cocktail

2 measures brandy
1 measure Cointreau
1 teaspoon anisette
ice

Shake vigorously in a cocktail shaker. Strain into a cocktail glass. Add a lump of ice.

Brandy Alexander

1 measure brandy
1 measure crème de cacao
1 measure fresh cream
ice

Shake with ice and strain into a champagne glass. Sprinkle freshly grated nutmeg on top.

Thunderclap

2 measures brandy
2 measures dry vermouth
1 teaspoon caster sugar
ice

Shake all the ingredients together. Strain into a cocktail glass.

TNT

2 measures brandy
1 measure orange curaçao
dash Pernod
dash of Angostura bitters
ice

Stir all the ingredients together in a mixing glass. Strain into a cocktail glass.

Brandy Applejack

2 measures of brandy
1 measure Calvados
1 measure Poire William
1 measure grenadine
1 measure lemon juice
ice

Shake all the ingredients together. Strain into a goblet half-filled with ice.

Sun and Shade

1 measure brandy
1 measure gin
ice

Shake all the ingredients together vigorously. Strain into a cocktail glass.

Thunder and Lightning

2 measures brandy
1 egg yolk
1 teaspoon caster sugar
cayenne pepper
ice

Combine all the ingredients in a shaker. Shake vigorously and strain into an old-fashioned glass. Sprinkle cayenne pepper on top.

Zoom

2 measures brandy
1 teaspoon honey
1 tablespoon boiling water
1 tablespoon heavy double cream
ice

Put the honey and boiling water into a shaker. Stir until the honey dissolves. Add the cream, brandy and ice. Shake vigorously. Strain into a cocktail glass.

Granada

2 measures brandy
1 measure dry sherry
1 teaspoon Cointreau
tonic water

Fill a highball glass with ice. Add the brandy, sherry and Cointreau. Stir well and top up with tonic water.

Rendezvous

1 measure brandy
1 measure strega
1 measure cherry brandy
pineapple spear
ice

Shake the ingredients well with the ice. Strain into a cocktail glass. Decorate with a pineapple spear.

Sir Henry

2 measures brandy
1 measure light rum
2 teaspoons Grand Marnier
1 teaspoon grenadine
1 teaspoon lemon juice
ice

Shake all the ingredients together vigorously with the ice cubes. Strain into a cocktail glass.

Moulin Rouge

2 measures brandy
3 measures pineapple juice
well-chilled sparkling white wine
ice

Half-fill a highball glass with ice. Pour in the brandy and pineapple juice. Stir and top up with the sparkling white wine.

April shower

2 measures brandy
1 measure Bénédictine
2 measures orange juice
soda water
ice

Half-fill a wine glass with ice. Add the brandy, Bénédictine and orange juice. Stir, then top up with soda water.

Andalusia

1 measure Spanish brandy
1 measure dry sherry
1 measure light rum
3 dashes Angostura bitters
ice

Put all the ingredients into a mixing glass. Stir well with the ice. Strain into a cocktail glass.

Mint Royal

1½ measures brandy
1½ measures Royal mint liqueur
1½ measures lemon juice
1 teaspoon egg white
sprig of mint
ice

Put all the ingredients into a shaker. Shake vigorously with ice. Strain into a cocktail glass. Decorate with sprig of mint.

4

FRUIT BRANDIES

Calvados

Of all fruit brandies produced, Calvados is by far the most famous. It is made in the apple-rich *département* of Calvados, located between St Malo and the Somme in Normandy, which has the delightful city of Caen as its capital. Calvados was named after a Spanish galleon the El Calvador which was found shipwrecked on the reefs off the Normandy coast in 1588. The region of production was first defined in 1949. There are 11 Calvados appellations. The best region, just east of Caen, is Vallée d'Auge and the appellation Pays d'Auge, around and inland from the town of Lisieux, is the best of all. Here the pot still, which leaves more flavouring elements in the finished spirit, is used. Other regions may use the continuous still which results in a lighter, less-defined product. Forty-eight different varieties of apples are used in the making of Calvados. They are graded from tart to sweet and in the Pays d'Auge only good-quality, high-grade fruit is used. Sometimes pears are added to bulk up the fruit.

Making Calvados

The fruit is crushed into a pulp and cultured yeast is added. When fermentation is completed the juice has been converted into cider. The cider is put into the pot still to undergo a double distillation. The first distillation produces 'low wines' also known as *petites eaux* or *brouíllis* with a main fraction of about 30 per cent alcohol. The second distillation produces a heart fraction – *alcools de coeur* – with an alcohol strength of about 60 per cent. The heads and tails, the first and final parts of the distillation, are sent back to be added to the oncoming cider for re-distillation.

Maturation

The heart, the new, raw, high-strength spirit is put into oak casks – often Limousin oak casks or sometimes old sherry or port casks – for maturation. The better qualities will be kept in wood for three to ten or more years, where they will take on a golden amber colour.

Label terminology

Indications of maturing age in cask are revealed on labels as follows:

Three stars means a minimum of two years maturing in cask.
Vieux or **Réserve** means a minimum of three years in cask.
VO or **Vieille Réserve** means a minimum of four years in cask.
VSOP means a minimum of five years in cask.
Hors d'Age or **Age Inconnu** means five years onwards in cask.

Drinking Calvados

Calvados is taken in the same way as brandy. A fine aged Calvados is a glorious drink and a wonderful way to end a meal. When drunk as a digestif it should be sipped and savoured. It is customary in northern France to drink Calvados between food courses or at the very least between the fish and main courses. Then it is drunk in one gulp to freshen the palate and make a hole (or space) for the rest of the meal – hence the expression *trou Normand* – the 'Norman holemaker'.

Well-known brands

Boulard
Château du Breuil
Dauphin
Père François

Busnel
Coeur de Lion
Gilbert
Père Magloire

——————— Applejack ———————

Applejack is an American apple brandy. It was first made in New England, with Connecticut the commercial centre. At that time the spirit was raw, fiery and very strong – so powerful indeed that when customers came into their local tavern they would ask for 'a slug of blue fish-hooks' or for 'lockjaw essence'. When the centre of trade moved to New Jersey the still-strong spirit became known as Jersey Lightning, because it packed a considerable wallop. Today, Applejack is a much more sophisticated product and is used in the same way as Calvados, as a digestif or for adding flavour to culinary dishes.

Making applejack

This spirit is distilled cider which has been made from the finest matured varieties of apples such as Granny Smith and Golden Delicious. The extracted juice of the apples goes through a slow, month-long, natural fermentation. The new cider is distilled twice in pot stills and the raw spirit is matured in charred oak barrels or in barrels made of Limousin oak, where it will remain for from two to ten years. During this time, the spirit will lose some of its alcohol strength and become gradually more smooth and mellow and softer in flavour. It will also extract some colour from the wood. It will be carefully appraised before being bottled.

Prestige brands

Bonny Doon (from Murphys, California)
Clear Creak (from Portland, Oregon)
Laird's (made from apples grown in the Delaware Valley; this famous company was established in 1780)

——— Brandy-associated drinks ———

Pineau des Charente

Pineau des Charente is a *vin de liqueur* made in the Cognac region. Its manufacture was the result of chance when a wine farmer accidentally tumbled grape juice into a barrel containing Cognac brandy.

This completely stopped fermentation and a sweet apéritif was born. It was first made on a commercial basis more than 400 years ago when Cognac producers found themselves with a surplus of brandy. There are two styles: white and rosé. White pineau uses the juice of the Ugni Blanc, Colombard, Sémillon and Meatils grapes. Rosé pineau is made from Cabernet Sauvignon, Cabernet Franc, Merlot and Malbec grapes.

Making pineau

The grapes get a light pressing and the juice is left to macerate with the grape extract and skins for a whole day. The juice is then removed and added in a three-to-one proportion to old Cognac which has an alcoholic strength of 60 per cent. The grape juice and the Cognac have to be produced in the same vineyard. No other additions are allowed. The new pineau is aged in cask for between one and two years, and before being bottled all pineau has to be sent to the Maison du Pineau for chemical and sensory tests. It should have an alcohol strength of between 16 and 22 per cent. Pineau des Charente is an adaptable drink. It can be taken on its own or with ice, or mixed with white wine, orange juice or tonic water. Although it is a recognised apéritif, it may also be taken during or after a meal.

Other wine apéritifs

Floc de Gascogne in red or white styles is a drink similar to pineau, but made in Armagnac using the local brandy. Another version is **Ratafia** made in Champagne.

In the Jura region of France a similar style of sweet wine apéritif is made, called **Macvin**. Red or white grape juice is blended with one third by volume of local *eau de vie de marc*. Some flavours such as cinnamon are added to spice it up.

———— Eaux de vie de fruits ————

Excellent fruit brandies are made in many locations, but principally in Alsace in France, the Black Forest area of Germany, in the former

Yugoslavia especially around Bosnia and in Switzerland. Most of the products are colourless and are known collectively by the French term *alcools blancs*.

Making eaux de vie de fruits

The fruit, be it plums, pears, peaches or whatever, is crushed into a pulp. This is fermented using cultured yeast and then it is double distilled in pot stills, a process which retains the congenerics or flavour agents of the original fruit. Because these brandies are water white and meant to be so, they are not aged in wood, which imparts some colour. Instead they are stored in large glass containers or immediately bottled to preserve their fresh flavours and fragrance.

When stone fruits are used, for example the plums used to make slivovitz or the cherries used in making kirsch, it is essential to add about one third of the crushed stone to the juice, as this imparts a fine, bitter-almond taste or tang to the final spirit. Some eaux de vie are made from soft fruits such as strawberries and raspberries and these are usually macerated in alcohol before distillation, especially so if the sugar content of the fruit is low. Often soft fruits of delicate flavour, will be left to macerate in neutral spirit for weeks. The spirit slowly extracts the flavours and no distillation is therefore necessary. These end up more like liqueurs than traditional eaux de vie.

In Germany two words *Wasser* and *Geist* reveal the methods of production. 'Wasser' as in **Kirschwasser** means that the spirit was produced from fermented fruit juice and then distilled. 'Geist' as in **Erdbeergeist** indicates that the fruit was macerated in alcohol and then distilled. It takes about 14 kg (30 lbs) of fruit to make one bottle of eau de vie.

Examples of eaux de vie

Name	Fruit used	Producing countries
Alisier	rowan berry	France
Barack Palinka	apricot	Hungary
Brombeergeist	blackberry	Germany and Switzerland
Cassis	blackcurrant	France

Erdbeergeist	strawberry	Germany and Switzerland
Fraises de Bois	wild strawberry	France
Framboise	raspberry	France
Himbeergeist	raspberry	Germany and Switzerland
Houx	holly berry	France
Kirschwasser	cherry	Germany and Switzerland
Mesclou	greengage	France
Mirabelle	yellow plum	France
Mûre Sauvage	wild blackberry	France
Myrtille	bilberry	France
Poire Williams	Williams pear	France, Switzerland and Germany
Prunelle	sloe	France
Quetsch	blue plum	France
Slivovitz	blue plum	Bosnia and Serbia
Tzuica	blue plum	Romania

Classic mixed drinks using Calvados as a base

Adam's Apple

1½ measures Calvados
¾ measure gin
¾ measure Italian vermouth
2 dashes yellow chartreuse
zest of a lemon
cherry
lemon peel
½ tumbler broken ice

Put all the ingredients into a mixing glass. Add the broken ice. Stir well and strain into a cocktail glass. Decorate with a cherry and a loop of lemon peel.

Applejack

2 measures Calvados
1 teaspoon orange curaçao
1 dash Angostura bitters
dash lemon juice
cherry
lemon peel
½ tumbler ice

Put all the ingredients into a mixing glass. Add the broken ice. Stir well and strain into a cocktail glass. Decorate with a cherry and a loop of lemon peel.

Beverly Hills

2 measures Calvados
2 dashes of Angostura bitters
dash of lemon juice
cherry
lemon peel
½ tumbler broken ice

Put all the ingredients into a mixing glass. Stir well and strain into a cocktail glass. Decorate with a cherry and a loop of lemon peel.

Honeyed Apples

2 measures Calvados
2 teaspoons honey
piping hot water

Mix the Calvados and honey in a heat-proof glass. Top up with the boiling water. Stir well.

Jack Rose

2 measures Calvados
1 measure lemon juice
1 teaspoon grenadine
dash zest of lemon
broken ice

Half-fill a shaker with broken ice. Add the ingredients. Shake well. Strain into a cocktail glass.

Riviera

1½ measures Calvados
1½ measures gin
1 dash grenadine
4 dashes lemon squash
slice of lemon
broken ice

Half-fill a shaker with broken ice. Add all the ingredients. Shake well. Strain into a small goblet. Decorate with a slice of lemon.

Rialto

1½ measures Calvados
1½ measures Italian red vermouth
2 dashes orange bitters
2 lumps sugar
2 sprigs mint
broken ice

Half-fill a mixing glass with broken ice. Add 1 sprig mint and the other ingredients. Stir very well and strain into a cocktail glass. Decorate with a slice of orange and a sprig of mint.

Star

1½ measures Calvados
1½ measures Italian red vermouth
1 teaspoon brown curaçao
2 dashes orange bitters
dash zest of lemon
slice of lemon
ice

Half-fill a mixing glass with broken ice. Then add the ingredients, stirring very well. Strain into a cocktail glass. Add a dash of lemon zest. Decorate with a slice of lemon.

5

GIN

A brief history of gin

Credit for the discovery of gin goes to a Dutch apothecary Franciscus de la Boe (1614–72). Dr Sylvius, as he was known, was Professor of Medicine at the University of Leyden in Holland. He had long recognised that the oils of juniper berries had diuretic values which helped flush out the urinary system, keeping the bladder and kidneys healthy. So he experimented with his medicinal tonic, mixing grain spirit with juniper-berry extract, and a rough-and-ready therapeutic but inexpensive medicine was born. He called it *geniévre*, the French for juniper (French was the polite language of the time). The Dutch renamed it *genever*, later it became known as geneva and subsequently the English anglicised it to gin.

English soldiers engaged in the 30 years war in the low countries of Europe sought solace in gin, especially before going into battle, and promptly dubbed it 'Dutch Courage'. Returning home they encouraged the production of the crude spirit. Soon gin became England's national drink. With the outbreak of war with France in 1688, the importation of French spirits ceased. Taxes on English-produced spirits were reduced in the reign of Queen Anne (1702–14) and this encouraged mass production of gin, most of it horrible stuff containing vitriolic ingredients. The cheapness and availability of the product led to widespread drunkenness and crime.

Gin gains in popularity

By 1729 recorded consumption soared to 5 million gallons (23 million litres) peaking to 11 million gallons (50 million litres) in 1750. During the period gin was sold openly on street corners and from barrows and stalls. Chemists also sold the dreadful stuff disguised in medicine bottles labelled 'colic water' and 'gripe water'. It was estimated at the time that one house in four in London sold gin. The spirit was so inexpensive that one owner of a 'strong water shop' in Southwark placed a notice outside which stated

Drunk for 1d (a penny)
Dead Drunk for 2d
Clean Straw for nothing

Hogarth's famous painting of Gin Lane in 1751 vividly shows the depravity and misery of the gin era. Idleness, vice and excess led, in many cases, to madness and worse.

Brand names began to appear including Cuckold's Comfort, Royal Poverty, Mother's Ruin, Last Shift, My Lady's Eye Water and the most popular of all, Old Tom. The latter was sold in London by Captain Dudley Bradstreet, a former government informer, whose job was to inform on the infringers of the law. In a rented house, he nailed the sign of a cat to his ground-floor window and put a lead pipe under the paw with a funnel attached inside. Passers-by were expected to put money in the cat's mouth and to ask 'Puss give me 2d worth of gin'. The liquid would come pouring out, giving the receiver a few generous mouthfuls. Could this have been the first coin-in-the-slot machine? It was a huge success, netting the captain £220 in a month – a fortune in those days.

Control of sales of gin

In 1751 the Gin Act, known as the 'Tippling Act', was introduced forbidding grocers, keepers of jails and workhouses from selling spirits. Henceforward, only people licensed by the Government could sell gin. This had a dramatic influence on the consumption of gin, which dropped from 11 million gallons (50 million litres) in the early 1750s to below 2 million gallons (9 million litres) by 1760. The temperance movement, together with more enlightened legislation regarding reasonable revenue duties on the manufacturers and, above all, the higher spirit prices charged to the consumer all contributed to the desired moderation in drinking. Professional distillers entered the business and, as the product improved and became more refined, three centres of production were established: London, Bristol and Plymouth. Taverns became popular and increasingly more comfortable, leading to the big, brassy but atmospheric 'gin palaces'. In 1871 an Act of Parliament tried to reduce the number of these premises by half. Public outrage ensured that the Act was quickly withdrawn.

In the 1880s the Americans introduced gin-based mixed drinks. The 1920s saw the dawn of the cocktail era, and many of the classic cocktails were gin based. Gin was considered respectable and was here to stay.

Styles of gin

There are two distinct styles of gin:

- **Dry gin**: English and American
- **Dutch gin**: Holland, Genever or Schiedam

Dry gin

Originally this style was known as London dry gin, indicating that it was the product of London gin distilleries. Today the name has no geographical significance and the style has been adopted in the United States and many other countries including Spain. The base neutral spirit is made from grain for the American market or from grain or molasses for the British and some European markets.

Gin is a flavoured spirit; the flavours are extracted from botanicals of which juniper berries are by far the most important and are always present wherever the gin is made. Choosing and buying the best botanicals is crucial to quality and consistency, as the final gin must taste exactly the same year in, year out. The botanicals are usually imported, and consist of:

- juniper berries from the Umbrian hillsides in Italy
- cardamom from the southern plains of India
- cinnamon from Ceylon
- coriander from the Crimea and Morocco

- angelica from Germany
- oranges and lemons from Spain and southern Italy
- cassia bark, orris roots and liquorice from the finest world markets.

Not all of these botanicals will be used. Each distillery has its own secret recipe. That, together with the distilling technique, the quality of the spirit and the quality of the water used in the reduction process, is the reason why brand-name gins taste slightly different from each other.

Making dry gin

There are four steps in the making of classical dry gin.

1 A low-strength wash is fermented from grain or molasses.
2 The wash is distilled in a patent still to produce an unrefined spirit.
3 This is rectified (re-distilled) in a patent still to elimate the poisonous higher alcohols. This purification removes all the congeners, resulting in a high-strength, colourless and flavourless neutral spirit.
4 The neutral spirit is put into a pot still. The flavouring agents are added and re-distilled with the flavourings impregnating the final spirit. Only the middle part of the distillate is bottled. The heads and tails are always sent back for rectification. Because of the purity of the spirit, gin does not require ageing. Once bottled, it is immediately ready for drinking.

Dutch gin

In the Netherlands, gin is made from a mash of malted barley, corn and rye. There are three steps in making Dutch gin.

1 The combination of grains is fermented into a 'beer'.
2 The 'beer' is distilled in pot stills and the distillate is re-distilled or rectified two or three times more. Then it is known as *Moutwijn* (malt wine).
3 The malt wine is now distilled with the botanicals in another pot still. Because it is distilled at a comparatively low proof strength, Dutch gin is very full bodied, rich and heavy flavoured.

Dutch gin has a definite malty aroma and taste; for that reason it is not a good mixer in cocktails, because its flavour would dominate the other ingredients. Ideally, it is drunk very cold and undiluted in small fridge-cooled glasses. Traditionally it is followed by a cold lager chaser.

Many Dutch gins are marketed in hand-made stone jars or crocks. Some are matured for a short time in Limousin oak casks before being bottled.

Alternative methods of making gin

- Some gins are made by adding the botanicals in concentrated form to the neutral spirit.
- The cheapest and poorest of all gins are made by the method known as 'cold compounding', where the neutral spirit is flavoured with essences and synthetic ingredients.

Popular brands of gin

United Kingdom
Beefeater
Bombay Sapphire
Booths
Coates (Plymouth)
Gordons
Tanqueray
Pavilion

Netherlands
Bols
De Kuyper
Notaris
Wenneker
Bokma
Hooghoudt

Belgium
Filliers
Hoorebeke
Meyboom
Peket de Houyeu

Spain
Larios
Rives Pitman

United States
Seagram's

Lithuania
Nemunas

Germany
Steinhäger

Ireland
Cork Dry Gin

——————————— # Drinking gin ———————————

Gin may be served neat, with ice, or with water or possibly with fruit juice. The popular gin and tonic was first experienced in British army messes in colonial India. A measure of quinine – to guard against malaria – would be mixed with aerated water and became known as Indian tonic water. The combination of gin and lime was introduced by the navy, as lime was used to keep scurvy at bay. Pink gin, another drink originating in the navy, uses Plymouth gin and a few drops of Angostura bitters. Then there are gin drinks with continental influence, gin and It (Italian sweet vermouth), gin and French (French dry vermouth). But for many, the favourite combinations are gin and tonic, refreshing whatever the weather and relaxing and comforting after work or play, or the stimulating Martini, also known as the Dry Martini cocktail.

How to make the perfect gin and tonic

Take a bottle of your favourite gin from the freezer. The alcohol content prevents the gin from freezing and the bottle from breaking. Use a good-quality tonic water, which should come straight from the fridge. Use freshly made clear, not cloudy, ice. Into a long glass that has also been chilled pour a decent measure of gin, top up with the tonic and ice. Add a slice of lemon or lime. As everything is cold the ice will not melt or dilute the drink.

The Martini

Nobody knows for certain who invented the Martini, considered by many to be the king of cocktails and the finest of all mixed drinks. Many writers on the subject give the credit to Martini di Arma di Taggia, Head Bartender in the Knickerbocker Hotel, New York City, around 1910. Apparently he invented the drink for his famously wealthy customer John D. Rockefeller using equal quantities of gin and French vermouth with an additional dash of orange bitters. Later he substituted the French vermouth with the dry vermouth of Martini & Rossi as a standard ingredient. Since those days no drink has generated more discussion or created more mystique than the Dry Martini cocktail. Connoisseurs of the drink – and they are legion – all seem to know a favourite bartender who mixes the best Martini in the world. Given opportunity they will propound on the merits of their preferred gin and its ratio to vermouth, and whether the drink tastes better shaken or stirred. Certainly the James Bond films have added to the controversy concerning how the drink should be made, but undoubtedly the films have also added to the prestige and popularity of the most sophisticated of all drinks.

The modern Martini has become increasingly drier and stronger, and the orange bitters flavour addition has virtually disappeared. The following recipe is wonderfully stimulating and conforms to contempory taste.

How to make the perfect Martini

1 generous measure of your favourite dry gin
⅓ of that volume of best-quality dry vermouth
shaving of lemon peel
plenty of ice cubes

Put the ice, gin and vermouth into a chilled mixing glass or glass jug. Stir vigorously with a spoon for 15 seconds. Strain into a Martini cocktail glass which has been taken straight from the fridge. Squeeze the sliver of lemon peel so that the zest falls on to the surface of the drink and creates a glaze. You can now drop the lemon peel into the drink or leave perfection as it is.

Types of gin

Fruit gins

Some gins are flavoured with orange or lemon or blackcurrant and have a certain following, especially in the Netherlands. Some are artificially flavoured.

London gin

The classic dry gin. The modern dry gins made in Britain and America are very similar.

Plymouth gin

More strongly flavoured with juniper berries than most gins and, by law, can be made only in the Black Friars Distillery that belongs to Coates and Company in Plymouth, Devon. It is a more assertive and aromatic gin than London gin and is the standard gin used in the making of a pink gin.

Dutch gin

Heavy and pungent to taste, principally because of the high malt content used in its preparation. It has a distinctive but clean flavour, you may see the words **Oude** (old) and **Jonge** (young) on labels. These terms have nothing to do with age. Oude is the original style usually straw-coloured, aromatic and slightly sweet. Jonge is lighter and drier and is the better-selling modern version.

German gin

Heavy flavoured and somewhat similar to Dutch gin. Steinhäger from Westphalia is a good example. It is marketed in stone flagons or crocks.

Old Tom gin

Now made in Scotland mainly for the export market. It is a sweetened London gin made by adding sugar syrup or glycerine to the finished gin.

Sloe gin

Made by steeping sloes, the fruit of the blackthorn, in gin. Sugar syrup and almonds are also added.

More classic mixed drinks using gin as a base

John Collins

1 measure gin
1 teaspoon sugar
juice of 1 lemon
1 dash Angostura bitters
soda water
ice

Put the ingredients except the soda water into a highball glass. Stir until the sugar is dissolved. Add soda water to taste. Decorate with a lemon slice.

Tom Collins is made in the same way as a John Collins but uses Old Tom gin, which is sweeter.

Horse's Neck

2 measures gin
dry ginger ale
ice

Place ice cubes and gin into a highball glass. Add ginger ale to taste. Decorate with a twist of lemon.

Clover Club

2 measures gin
1 measure grenadine
juice of ½ lemon
¼ egg white
ice

Shake thoroughly with ice in a shaker. Strain into a large cocktail glass. Decorate with lemon peel and a cherry.

Pink Lady

2 measures gin
1 teaspoon grenadine
¼ white of egg
ice

Shake with ice and strain into a large cocktail glass.

Negroni

1 measure gin
1 measure sweet vermouth
1 measure Campari
ice

Stir all the ingredients together in mixing glass with ice. Strain into a rocks glass. Decorate with lemon peel.

Bronx

1 measure gin
½ measure dry vermouth
½ measure sweet vermouth
1 measure fresh orange juice
ice

Shake with ice and strain into a rocks glass. Decorate with a slice of orange.

Fibber McGee

1½ measures dry gin
½ measure unsweetened grapefruit juice
½ measure sweet Italian vermouth
2 dashes Angostura bitters
twist lemon rind
ice

Stir ingredients with ice in a mixing glass. Strain into a cocktail glass. Add a twist of lemon rind.

Codswallop

1½ measures gin
⅛ measure Campari
⅛ measure raspberry liqueur
⅛ measure lime juice
4 measures lemonade
ice

Put all the ingredients into a tall ice-filled glass. Stir very gently.

Superman

1 measure gin
¾ measure dry vermouth
½ measure apricot brandy
1 measure mandarin juice
1 teaspoon grenadine
broken ice

Shake all ingredients together with a glassful of broken ice. Pour unstrained into a rocks glass.

César Ritz

2 measures gin
⅔ measure dry vermouth
⅛ measure cherry brandy
⅛ measure kirsch
red cherry for decoration
ice

Put all ingredients in a mixing glass. Mix with ice and strain into a cocktail glass. Decorate with a red cherry that has been soaked in eau de vie.

Caruso

1 measure gin
1 measure dry vermouth
1 measure green crême de menthe
cherry for decoration
broken ice

Add the ingredients to a rocks glass half-filled with broken ice. Stir, decorate with a cherry on a stick. If white crême de menthe is used the drink is then called **Caruso Blanco**.

White Lady

1 measure dry gin
½ measure Cointreau
½ measure fresh lemon juice
ice

Shake the ingredients together with ice. Strain into a cocktail glass.

Old Etonian

1 measure gin
1 measure lillet
2 dashes crême de noyau
2 dashes orange bitters
orange peel for garnish
ice

Shake the ingredients together with ice. Strain into a cocktail glass. Squeeze orange peel on top.

Pink Gin

1½ measures Plymouth gin
several drops Angostura bitters
iced water or soda water

Shake several drops of Angostura bitters into a wine goblet. Roll the bitters around the glass. Shake out any surplus. Pour the gin into the glass. Add ice or iced water or soda water according to individual taste.

Singapore Gin Sling

2 measures dry gin
½ measure Cointreau
½ measure cherry brandy
juice of 1 lemon
heaped teaspoon powdered sugar
soda water
slice of lemon
ice

Put ice cubes into a large, tall glass. Add the gin, lemon juice and sugar. Now add Cointreau and cherry brandy. Top up with soda water. Stir gently. Decorate with a slice of lemon and serve with two straws.

South of the Border

1½ measures dry gin
1 measure fresh lemon juice
1 measure kahlúa
1 teaspoon egg white
ice

Shake the ingredients together vigorously with the ice. Strain into a cocktail glass. Decorate with a cocktail cherry.

Silver Streak

1 measure gin
½ measure kümmel
½ measure fresh lemon juice
ice

Shake all ingredients togther with ice. Strain into a cocktail glass.

Orange Blossom

1½ measures gin
1½ measures orange juice
½ teaspoon caster sugar
ice

Shake all ingredients together with ice. Strain into a wine goblet filled with crushed ice. Decorate with an orange slice and a cherry.

Gloom Chaser

1½ measures dry gin
1 measure dry vermouth
½ teaspoon grenadine
2 dashes Pernod
ice

Shake all ingredients together with ice. Strain into a cocktail glass.

Ideal

1 measure dry gin
½ measure dry vermouth
½ measure fresh grapefruit juice
1 teaspoon powdered sugar
2 dashes Angostura bitters
ice

Shake all ingredients together with ice. Strain into a cocktail glass. Decorate with a cocktail cherry.

Beef on Rye

1½ measures Beefeaters gin
½ measure Canadian rye whisky
½ measure passion fruit syrup
2 measure sparkling bitter lemon
ice

Put all the ingredients except the bitter lemon into a shaker. Shake with ice cubes and strain into a rocks glass half-filled with broken ice. Now add the sparkling bitter lemon.

Eclipse

1½ measures sloe gin
½ measure dry gin
½ measure grenadine
1 red cherry
ice

Put all the ingredients except the cherry and grenadine into a shaker. Shake with ice and strain the gins into a small goblet containing the cherry. Gently add the grenadine to cover the cherry at the bottom of the glass.

6

ABSINTHE AND PASTIS

Absinthe

Absinthe was created in the eighteenth century by Dr Ordinaire, a French physician and pharmacist in Couvet, Switzerland. The spirit was flavoured with many aromatic herbs grown in the Jura mountains. These included aniseed, coriander, fennel, hyssop, liquorice, orris root and, most importantly, wormwood (*Artemisia absinthium*) which was the inspiration for the drink's names. The drink was powerful and deleterious, green in colour with a dry and bitter taste. It became so popular in France and Switzerland in the 1890s that the apéritif hour became known as *l'heure vert*. Elsewhere the drink was known as the Green Goddess or Green Muse.

The drink was marketed by Henry Louis Pernod, and after Dr Ordinaire's death the recipe was sold to the Pernod family. They started to produce the drink at Pontarlier, close to the Swiss border, and established 22 absinthe distilleries in the locality. But absinthe was to gain a wretched reputation. It was blamed for the high level of alcoholism in France, and the potency of the drink – 68 per cent alcohol – combined with the herb wormwood was considered lethal. When taken neat absinthe was said to drive people mad or to suicide. Consequently its production was outlawed in Switzerland in 1907, and the drink was banned in the United States in 1912 and in France in 1915. Other countries followed and denounced the product, but Pernod took the recipe, which they acquired in 1795, to Tarragona in Spain and established a distillery. Absinthe is still made legally and commercially there.

Pastis

Pastis is the generic name for aniseed-flavoured spirits of various origins. The aniseed may be produced in the South of France, in Spain, Turkey, Greece or in North Vietnam. These spirits have characteristics common to absinthe, but they are lower in alcohol and are not flavoured with the controversial wormwood, which caused absinthe to be banned. In appearance these drinks are usually colourless but they turn opalescent or milky when water is added. The addition of water brings the volatile oils in the drink out of solution into suspension. Pastis is particularly popular in countries bordering the Mediterranean. **Pernod** and **Ricard** are the market leaders in France where they are known as Pastis de Marseilles. Other countries make their own individual styles. Spain makes **ojen**, Greece **ouzo** and **mastikha**, Turkey makes **raki** and Italy **anice**. France also makes non-alcoholic versions called **Blancard** and **Pacific**.

Drinking pastis

Pour a measure of pastis into a goblet. Pour over iced water. The usual proportion is three parts water to one of pastis.

In the past the traditional service of pastis was much more complicated. A silver filter containing a lump of ice and a cube of sugar was placed over the glass and the water was then dripped through the filter into the measure of pastis. The sugar was there to sweeten the drink. This is no longer necessary as modern pastis is already sweetened.

Arrack

Arrack or arak gets its names from the Arabic word *araq* meaning 'juice' or 'sweat'. It is a highly potent drink made from a variety of raw materials. It is produced mainly in the Middle East and Far East. In Iraq and Egypt it is made from dates, and from grapes in the Lebanon and Syria. In Turkey and the Balkans where it is known as **raki**, it is variously made from potatoes, plums, molasses, rice and the fermented sap of the coconut palm. Arrack is a powerful, white alcohol, and in the Middle East it is served accompanied by a plate of *maza* – a selection of titbits consisting of a variety of radishes, cheese and hard-boiled eggs. The suggestion is that if you don't have food to accompany the drink your equilibrium will be affected. The drink is often flavoured with aniseed, which makes it a form of pastis.

Batavia arak is quite different. It is a brandy-like rum made from molasses on the island of Java in Indonesia, and flavoured with little cooked cakes of Javanese red rice which are added before distillation to the fermenting molasses. When distilled the arak is very pungent and highly aromatic. It is aged in wood for four to six years, and is very popular in Sweden where it forms the base for their famous Arrack Punsch.

Bitters

Bitters are spirits flavoured with herbs, spices, barks, roots and fruits. Their exact formulae are trade secrets, but they were originally made as medicines and elixirs. Some are taken as correctifs or hangover drinks. Most are used as apéritifs or in cocktail and mixed-drinks recipes. Many can have an alcohol content as high as 40 per cent or more. But the one thing they all have in common is bitterness.

Best-known bitters

Angostura

Angostura was the inspiration of a German doctor, J. G. B. Siegert. He served as a surgeon with the Prussian army and was a veteran of the Napoleonic wars. He went to Venezuela to help Simón Bolívar liberate Bolivia from the Spanish, and settled in a Venezuelan town called Angostura, where he invented his aromatic 'medicine' in 1824. By 1830 the bitters was being marketed worldwide. In 1846 the town of Angostura was renamed Cíudad Bolivar. With the death of Siegert in 1870 and the worsening political climate in Venezuela, the Siegert sons decided in 1875 to move the business to Trinidad, and Angostura has been made there ever since. Angostura has a base of rum and is flavoured with gentian and vegetable spice. Its alcohol content is 44.7 per cent. It is a favoured ingredient in many cocktails and mixed drinks, and it is often used to add flavour to soups and sauces.

Amer Picon

This is a French bitters, an extract of distilled spirit, quinine, oranges and herbs. It was invented in 1835 by a French army officer, Gaston Picon, as an antidote to malaria. It is especially popular in France where it is drunk as an apéritif with gin or with soda and ice.

Campari

Campari is a very popular bitters and more pleasant to drink than most other bitters. It is vivid red in colour and is usually taken with ice, soda and a slice of lemon or orange. You must stir the drink or the ingredients will separate. There are also two classic cocktails made with Campari. One is the Americano which is made up of equal measures of Campari and red Italian vermouth with ice and soda water added. The other is Negroni which consists of equal parts of Campari, sweet red Italian vermouth and gin (see Chapter 5). All the ingredients are stirred well and chilled with ice cubes. Campari is the world's best-selling bitters. It was first produced in Milan in 1862 by Gaspere Campari, a famous restaurateur. Alcohol content is 25 per cent.

Echt Stonsdorfer

This was created in Germany by the distiller Christian Koerner in 1810. This bitters is made from 43 different ingredients including wood-blueberries. It has a fruity, bitter taste.

Fernet Branca

This has been made in Milan since 1845, but it is now also made under licence in France, Switzerland, the United States and Argentina. The recipe calls for 30 different herbs and roots including Chinese rhubarb, gentian, camomile, saffron and ginger. These are steeped in white wine and brandy and the infusion is aged in cask for at least a year.

Branca Menta

A more palatable mint-flavoured version of the brand, it is usually drunk as a Highball, that is with soda water or ginger ale. Both styles have an alcoholic strength of 40 per cent.

Gammel Dansk Bitter Dram

This is made in Roskilde, Denmark, from 29 ingredients including gentian and rowan berries. It is the biggest-selling spirit in Denmark.

Ramazzotti

This Italian bitters was first made in Milan in 1815 by herbalist Ausano Ramazzotti. He infused 33 different roots and herbs in alcohol. The ingredients include gentian, angelica, chinchona bark, anise, iris and fruit peel.

Riga Black Balsam

A popular Latvian bitters, this was first produced in the eighteenth century by a pharmacist from Riga called Abraham Kunze. It is made from 16 ingredients which include raspberries, mint, honey, wormwood and the blossom of lime trees. It has a high alcohol content of 45 per cent and is sold in attractive ceramic bottles.

Underberg

Underberg is promoted as an aid to digestion, but it is also to be recommended as an apéritif or as a hangover cure. Hubert Underberg formulated his company in Rheinberg, Germany, in 1846. He created his elixir from choice aromatic herbs which are carefully selected from 43 countries. These are blended with brandy and left to mature in barrels of Slovenian oak for many months. In 1940 the drink was first sold in tiny bottles holding single-nip portions of 2 centilitres. You are meant to swallow the contents in one gulp – or you may prefer to add soda water as Underberg has an alcoholic strength of 45 per cent. Underberg is now also produced in Zurich and Vienna.

Zwack Unicum

This famous Hungarian bitters was created by Jozsef Zwack in 1790. Following the takeover of Hungary by the communists the Zwacks went into exile in 1942 in the United States and Unicum was then made in Italy. In 1990 Peter Zwack returned to Hungary where Unicum is made once again from the original recipe using 40 botanicals. The alcohol strength is 42 per cent.

Other well-known bitters

Abbott's Aged Bitters (prepared since 1865 in Baltimore, USA, by the Abbott family)
Peychaud's (made in New Orleans, USA)
Amaro Montenegro, China Martini and **Radis** (all from Italy)
Boonekamp and **Welling** (from the Netherlands)
Amara (from South America)
Arquebuse, Secrestat, Suze and **Toni-Kola** (from France)
Calisaya (from Spain)
Orange bitters (flavoured with the dried peel of bitter Seville oranges) and peach bitters (made from peach kernels) are used in some cocktail and mixed-drink recipes.

———— Aquavit/schnapps ————

Aquavit or akvavit is native to Denmark, Sweden, Norway and Iceland and is also popular in Germany. The name is a contraction of *aqua vitae* meaning 'water of life'. It is also known as schnaps in Denmark, snaps in Norway and Sweden, and schnapps in Germany. These latter names mean gasp or snatch, which is the usual reaction when the ice cold drink is swallowed in one gulp. It is perhaps the perfect drink to accompany Smørgasbord, the wonderful and exotic cold buffet foods of Scandanavia, because it cuts right through the oily content of the food. In Germany it is often served with cocktail bites such as canapes and roll mops. It is a stimulating drink at parties, as it helps to make people relax. On formal occasions it is customary in Scandinavia to drink as many toasts as there are buttons on a man's jacket. The toasting ceremony is accompanied by the ritual of staring into your neighbour's eyes with glasses held chest high as the drink goes down.

Making of aquavit/schnapps

The basic fermented wash is obtained from potatoes or grain. This is distilled in a patent still, re-distilled and then filtered through layers of vegetable charcoal to make it absolutely pure. Finally it is flavoured with caraway, cardamom, cumin, dill, fennel and citrus peel. Aquavit is not matured, but as it emerges from the still it is filtered and reduced in strength. It may be held in a glass-lined container for a resting or settling period before it is bottled for sale.

Drinking aquavit

Aquavit is served straight from the freezer into small glasses which have been chilled in the fridge. If preferred, the ice-cold drink can be followed by a lager or beer chaser. In Germany hardened drinkers like to swallow a few shots of schnapps before settling into a session of beer drinking. They say the spirit warms the stomach in preparation for the cold beer. One of the most interesting and better-quality aquavits is the Norwegian brand, Linie. The line in the brand name refers to the equator. It is traditional that the spirit is carried in American oak casks on board Wilhelmsen liners, as they sail over the equator on their voyages to and from Australia. The custom started over a century ago when it was noticed that the movement of the ship, combined with the different temperatures experienced, made the spirit more smooth and mellow and caused it to take on a pale golden colour. Since 1985 aquavit has been transported even further, but always via Australia, as the ships make round-the-world voyages.

Well-known brands

Aalborg Taffel (from Denmark)   O. P. Anderson (from Sweden)
Aalborg Jubilaeums (from Denmark)   Bommerlünder (from Germany)
Lysholm Linie (from Norway)   Suktinis (from Lithuania)
Loitens Export (from Norway)   Zalgiris (from Lithuania)

Kornbranntwein

Kornbranntwein or corn brandy is a German speciality. It is somewhat similar to a light grain whiskey in flavour. As the name suggests it is made from *Korn* (maize) and the *Kornsprit* (neutral spirit) is often flavoured, which then makes it into another variety of schnapps. Flavouring may include juniper berries (*Wachholderkornbrannt*) and apples (*Apfelkorn*), even pears, grapefruit and oranges are sometimes preferred. There are two distinct products: **Korn** which has an alcohol strength of 32 per cent vol and the much stronger **Doppelkorn** – 38 to 45 per cent vol. Korn is served straight from the fridge into small glasses, it is taken neat.

Well-known brands of Korn

Alter Koerner   Fürst Bismarck
Berentzen Apfel   Kornelius
Doornkat

7

TEQUILA

Tequila is the national spirit of Mexico. It is made from the blue agave plant of the genus *Amaryllis*. It is perhaps better known as the century plant and is sometimes called the argarth, maguey or mezcal. Although there are many varieties of the agave plant, by law, true tequila can be made only when the blue agave is grown in the state of Jalisco. The distillation usually takes place in or near the town of Tequila, which is located just north-west of Guadalajara.

It takes 8 to 12 years for the plant to reach maturity. By then, the plant will have grown to 1.5 m (5 feet) or more. When harvested, the sticky, yucca-style leaves are cut away leaving the base which looks like a giant pineapple. This is known as the pina or heart and weighs 36 to 50 kg (80 to 110 lbs). When removed, only a stump remains in the ground. The pina will be heavy with a sweet sap called *aguamiel* (honey water) and each pina will yield about 27 litres (6 gallons) of spirit.

Making tequila

At the distillery, the pinas are split into chunks and steam-cooked for 48 hours to convert the starches into fermentable sugars. These are extracted by crushing and then running water through the pina. After fermentation of the aguamiel, the resultant 'wine', called pulque, is distilled twice in pot stills giving a pure, white spirit of an approximate alcohol strength of 50 per cent.

Grading

Tequila is graded according to the length of time the spirit has matured in oak casks.

Silver is the standard tequila and gets no ageing (or very little) in cask.
Reposado is aged up to six months in cask.
Gold is aged for varying periods in cask, but its colour is often enhanced by the addition of caramel.
Añejo is aged from one to three years and is usually the best-quality and the most expensive tequila.

By law, tequila must contain a minimum of 51 per cent agave spirit with cane spirit making up the balance. However, 100 per cent agave tequilas are always obtainable. Look for the NOM number (Norma Oficial Mexicans de Calidad) on labels. This guarantees that the particular brand has adhered to quality-production regulations.

———— Drinking tequila ————

Shooting The conventional method of drinking tequila is attended with appropriate ritual. A pinch of salt is placed on the back of the hand between thumb and forefinger. The same thumb and forefinger then hold a slice of lime. The other hand holds a shot glass of tequila. First, take a lick of the salt, then shoot the tequila down your throat in one gulp and bite into the lime.

Slamming A tequila slammer is a mixture of tequila and sparking wine or lemonade. The chosen combination is put into a glass and covered by your hand or by a napkin. The glass is slammed down on to a counter top or table, and as the contents froth and foam, you slam them down your throat.

Perhaps the best way of all to enjoy tequila, is to order or make a Margarita (see page 102). Legend has it that Margarita was the beautiful, dark-haired girlfriend of a Mexican barman. She was gunned down by a stray bullet during a bar-room brawl. The barman created the drink in her memory.

Some bars offer even more personalised service in the shape of tequila girls who come fully equipped to mix or slam at your table. They wear customised leather belts, after the fashion of Mexican bandits. Shot glasses are stored where bullets used to be and the holsters holds a bottle of tequila on one side and a bottle of sparkling wine on the other.

Well-known brands of tequila

It was a Spaniard, Don José Maria Guadalupe Cuervo, who first commercialised the production of tequila in 1795. **José Cuervo** is still family owned and the brand is the market leader, followed by other classic brands such as **Herradura**, **Mariachi**, **Montezuma**, **Olmeca**, **Pepe Lopez**, **Saliza** and **Sierra**.

Mezcal

Mezcal is a spirit related to tequila as it is also made from the agave. However, it is made from various species of the agave which do not have to be grown in the delimited tequila zone. The mezcal pina is cooked in a wood-fired oven which imparts a smoky flavour, retained right through to the finish. The juice and some of the fibrous material of the pina is fermented and the extract is distilled once in a pot still. It gets little or no ageing and is the traditional drink of native Mexicans. It is often bottled with an agave worm inside the bottle. The grub is purposely put there to attract attention and to prove that the drink is sufficiently strong in alcohol to preserve the worm. Mezcal has a bitter almond taste and is usually taken neat.

Classic mixed drinks using tequila as a base

Acapulco

1 measure tequila
1 measure Tia Maria
1 measure dark rum
150 ml (5 fl oz) coconut cream
ice
Shake with ice and strain into a rocks glass.

Tequila Sunrise

2 measures tequila
orange juice
1 teaspoon grenadine
ice

Fill a highball glass with ice cubes. Add tequila and enough orange juice to within 12 mm (½ inch) of the top. Add the grenadine and decorate with orange and a cherry. Drink through straws.

Margarita

1 measure tequila
1 measure Cointreau or Curaçao
2 teaspoons lime juice
lemon
salt
ice

Shake the tequila, Cointreau or Curaçao and lime juice together with ice. Rub the rim of a cocktail glass with lemon to moisten. Dip the glass rim into a saucer of fine salt. Strain the cocktail into the prepared glass.

Icebreaker

2 measures tequila
1 tablespoon grenadine
1 measure grapefruit juice
2 teaspoons Cointreau
crushed ice

Mix the ingredients in a blender at low speed and strain into a sour glass.

Eldorado

2 measures tequila
1½ measures lemon juice
1 tablespoon honey
crushed ice

Shake well with crushed ice and strain into a Collins glass. Add two ice cubes.

Earthquake

2 measures tequila
1 teaspoon grenadine
2 drops of Cointreau
2 strawberries
crushed ice

Mix the ingredients in a blender with crushed ice. Strain into a
cocktail glass. Decorate with a strawberry and orange slice.

Sloes in Heaven

1½ measures tequila
1 measure sloe gin
½ measure Italian red vermouth
ice

Three-quarters fill an old-fashioned glass with ice cubes. Pour in all
the ingredients. Stir well and decorate with a slice of lemon.

The Rising Sun

1½ measures tequila
1½ measures pisang ambon
dash of blue curaçao
ice

Put the tequila and pisang ambon into a mixing glass with ice. Stir
and strain into a champagne flute glass. Slowly drip the blue curaçao
through the centre of the cocktail to get an attractive two-tone effect.

Dodo

1 measure tequila
1 measure mezcal
½ measure blue curaçao
pinch icing sugar
soda water or tonic water
ice

Have a large wine glass frosted with blue sugar ready. Pour the tequila,
mezcal and blue curaçao in a shaker. Add the icing sugar and ice.
Shake. Strain into the prepared glass. Top up with soda water or
tonic water.

Chocolate Full Moon

2 measures tequila
½ measure dark crème de cacao
½ measure light crème de cacao
1 measure fresh cream
ice

Put all the ingredients into a shaker. Shake well with the ice. Strain into a cocktail glass. Decorate with a pinch of grated chocolate.

Copa de Oro

1 measure tequila
1 measure Grand Marnier
1 teaspoon sugar
1 egg
cracked ice

Shake all the ingredients together vigorously with craked ice. Strain into a wine goblet, its top covered by a round of orange with two straws protruding through it.

Jarana

2 measures tequila
2 teaspoons powdered sugar
pineapple juice
ice

Put plenty of ice cubes in a tall glass. Add the ingredients and stir well. Top up with pineapple juice.

Cactus Juice

2 measures gold tequila
1 teaspoon Drambuie
1 measure fresh lemon juice
1 teaspoon caster sugar
broken ice

Put all the ingredients in a shaker. Shake with broken ice. Pour unstrained into a rocks glass.

Brave Bull

1 measure gold tequila
1 measure kahlúa
broken ice

Add the ingredients to a rocks glass filled with broken ice. Stir and decorate with a twist of lemon.

If served without the ice, and a flaming teaspoon of Sambuca is floated on top, the drink then becomes a **Raging Bull**.

Tequila Exotica

1½ measures tequila
¼ measure white crême de cacao
1 teaspoon curaçao
1 measure mango juice
1 measure white grape juice
½ measure fresh lime juice
ice

Put all the ingredients into a shaker. Shake with ice cubes. Strain into a rocks glass three-quarters filled with broken ice. Decorate with half an orange slice and a green grape.

Tequila Slammer

1 measure gold tequila
1 measure cold lemonade or ginger ale or sparkling wine

Add the ingredients to a small tumbler known as a shot glass. Cover the glass with your hand or a napkin or a beer mat. Rap the glass twice on the table and drink immediately while the drink is fizzing.

8
VODKA

A brief history of vodka

Vodka originated in the twelfth century, either in Russia or Poland, and its popularity quickly spread throughout the Baltic states. It takes its name from the Russian *Zhiznennia Voda* meaning 'water of life'. It has appeared under such names as wódka, wodki, vodki, vidky and now vodka. Translated the name means 'little water' because like water, it is colourless, tasteless and odourless. Like gin, vodka was first made for medicinal purposes as a cure for gout, gallstones and fragile stomachs. The basic raw material came from many vegetable sources, cane, grain and potatoes. What was used depended on the product with the largest annual surplus.

Vodka gains popularity

Although vodka is native to European countries, it is now made in many other countries worldwide. The Americans really made the drink fashionable. The vogue for vodka started in the 1940s in California and swept the country when it was realised that vodka was such a natural companion for mixed drinks and cocktails. About this time a new drink in The Cock'n Bull Tavern in Los Angeles was created which was to take America by storm. It was called Moscow Mule – a combination of vodka, ginger beer and a little lime juice. The vodka used was Smirnoff which was now made and marketed by the US firm Hueblein. The company gave heavy promotion to vodka and Moscow Mule in particular.

Surprisingly, this drinking revolution did not make much impact in Western Europe. Britain was especially slow to accept vodka's qualities. However, Russian and Polish émigrés fleeing the Russian Revolution helped to create a demand. Since then, there has been a proliferation of brands with marketing aimed at young people who find that vodka is a pleasurable, easy introduction to spirits. It also has the added attraction that it can be 'felt, not smelt'. Vodka is a clean spirit, it has a youthful image and it is a great mixer. It is also claimed that vodka is less fattening and less conducive to hangovers than other spirits.

Controls on vodka

Excessive drinking of vodka has been a continuing problem in the former Soviet Union. Russia, in fact, banned the making of the spirit between 1914 and 1925. When production was restored, ostensibly for medicinal purposes, the nation was once again submerged in the gloom of alcohol excess. In 1985 Mr Gorbachov tried to repair the damage to health and productivity by curtailing the manufacture of vodka and the times that it was legally available for sale. But old habits die hard and the people continued to resort to vodka as an escape.

Making vodka

The base raw material chosen to be fermented into a wash comes from a variety of vegetable products, chiefly grain, potatoes or molasses. The choice often depends on the material most plentiful and least expensive. The wash is distilled and then rectified in a patent still. This results in an almost pure spirit, which is then slowly passed through layers of vegetable charcoal or activated carbon to remove any remaining traces of colour and flavour to achieve complete neutrality.

Drinking vodka

Traditionally when Russians and Poles open a bottle of vodka, it is never put away half empty. They drink it with indecent speed because they believe that by sipping it you inhale more alcohol than you drink. Vodka is best taken very cold in small tumblers which have come straight from the freezer – 'with a tear' as the Russians say. The glasses will be frosted with the intense cold and the tears will form on the outside. Served in this manner, vodka is drunk in one straight gulp. Like that, it is certainly the drink that will leave you breathless until the warm inner glow takes over. In restaurants, vodka is often presented with the bottle or carafe encased up to the neck in ice. Besides being attractive, the presentation ensures that the vodka is kept at the ideal temperature. A more leisurely way to drink vodka is with mixers (e.g. tonic water) over ice, or with fresh orange juice (Screwdriver), or with ginger beer (Moscow Mule), or with tomato juice (Bloody Mary, see page 110).

Flavoured vodkas

Although vodkas are generally unflavoured, there are some flavoured varieties also available, especially in Russia and Poland. Popular flavours include rowan berry, lemon, peppers, honey and cherries. Some vodkas are even coloured using sunflower seeds to give a hint of mauve, saffron for yellow, cornflowers for blue, walnut shells for brown and *Zubrówka* grass to give a suggestion of green. Incidentally, the Polish Zubrówka is one of the great vodkas. It is made with an infusion of zubrówka grass – the grass that European bison or buffalo graze on. It is delicately aromatic, with a slightly nutty flavour. A long blade of the grass floats inside each bottle.

Well-known brands

Russia	Krepkaya	**Finland**	Finlandia
	Limonnaya		Koskenkorva
	Moskovskaya	**Sweden**	Absolut
	Starka	**United States**	Wolfschmidt
	Stolichnaya	**Ireland**	Saratof
	Zubrovka		Nordoff
Poland	Bielska	**Siberia**	Sibirskaya
	Jarzebiak	**Ukraine**	Gorilka
	Karpatia	**Germany**	Gorbatschow
	Starka	**Estonia**	Eesti Viin
	Wyborowa		Viru Valge
	Zubrówka	**Wales**	Raw Spirit
United Kingdom	Cossak		
	Smirnoff		

Classic mixed drinks using vodka as a base

Moscow Mule

1½ measures vodka
juice of ½ lemon
ginger beer
ice

Fill a highball glass with ice, add the vodka and lime juice. Top up with ginger beer to taste. Stir and decorate with a slice of lime.

Vodkatini

1 measure vodka
1 dash dry sherry
ice

Stir together all the ingredients. Strain into a cocktail glass and decorate with lemon peel.

Harvey Wallbanger (Screwdriver with Galliano)

2 measures vodka
Galliano
fresh orange juice
ice

Fill a highball glass with ice. Add vodka and enough orange juice to fill the glass to within 12 mm (½ inch) from the top. Float over the Galliano on the back of a spoon. Decorate with an orange slice.

Black Russian

2 measures vodka
1 measure kahlúa or other coffee liqueur
ice

Stir all the ingredients together. Strain and serve in a cocktail glass.

Screwdriver

1 measure vodka
fresh orange juice
ice

Fill a rocks glass with ice. Add vodka, top up with orange juice and stir. Decorate with a slice of orange.

Bloody Mary

2 measures vodka
150 ml (5 fl oz) tomato juice
2 dashes Worcestershire sauce
2 dashes lemon juice
1 dash Tabasco sauce
1 pinch celery salt
slight sprinkle of cayenne pepper
ice

Stir together all the ingredients in a highball glass with ice. Decorate with mint and a celery stick.

Bullshot

1 measure vodka
3 measures condensed beef stock
2 measures tomato juice
dash lime juice
dash Worcestershire sauce
dash chilli sauce
ground pepper and celery salt
ice

Put all the ingredients in a shaker. Shake well. Pour into a highball glass half-filled with ice. Decorate with a slice of cucumber and two cherry tomatoes.

Road Runner

2 measures vodka
1 measure Amaretto liqueur
2 measures coconut milk
nutmeg
ice

Place all the ingredients in a shaker. Shake vigorously with ice. Strain into a cocktail glass. Add a dusting of grated nutmeg on top.

Galway Gray

1½ measures vodka
1 measure white crême de cacao
1 measure Cointreau
½ measure lime juice
fresh cream
ice

Stir all the ingredients except the cream together. Strain into a cock-tail glass. Using the back of teaspoon, float the cream on top of the drink. Garnish with grated orange peel.

Salty Dog

2 measures vodka
fresh grapefruit juice
ice

Prepare a highball glass frosted with salt. Put the ice in the salt-frosted glass. Pour in the vodka. Top up with the grapefruit juice. Decorate with a wedge of lemon.

Blue Lagoon

1½ measures vodka
1½ measures blue curaçao
lemon-lime soda
ice

Pour the vodka and curaçao into a long-stemmed goblet filled with ice. Stir and top up with the lemon-lime soda. Decorate with cocktail cherries.

Sea Waves

1½ measures vodka
½ measure dry vermouth
½ measure blue curaçao
½ measure Galliano
ice

Pour the ingredients into a wine goblet half-filled with ice cubes. Stir well and decorate with maraschino cherries.

Surf Rider

2 measures vodka
1 measure sweet vermouth
juice of one orange
squeeze of lime
1 teaspoon grenadine
ice

Pour all the ingredients into a shaker. Shake well and strain into a wine goblet. Decorate with a slice of orange and a maraschino cherry.

White Russian

1 measure vodka
½ measure kahlúa
½ measure white crême de cacao
1 measure fresh cream
grated chocolate
nutmeg
ice

Shake all the ingredients thoroughly with cracked ice. Strain into a highball glass half-filled with ice cubes. Decorate with freshly grated-chocolate and nutmeg.

Fuzzy Navel

1 measure vodka
1 measure peach schnapps
4 measures freshly squeezed orange juice
ice

Put all the ingredients into a highball glass half-filled with ice. Decorate with a slice of peach and a slice of orange.

Patricia

1 measure vodka
1 measure sweet red Italian vermouth
1 measure Cointreau
ice

Stir the ingredients with ice in a cocktail glass. Decorate with a twist of orange peel.

9
RUM

A brief history of rum

Rum is made wherever the sugar cane grows freely. It is the by-product of sugar production and the Caribbean is its natural home. The names comes from 'rumbullion' or 'rumbustion', two words used in the West Indies, or alternatively from the Latin word for sugar, *saccharum*.

Christopher Columbus brought the sugar cane to the West Indies in 1493. He took cane cuttings from the Canary Islands and planted them in Hispaniola – now the Dominican Republic and Haiti. Soon sugar was being produced throughout the Caribbean, but there was one snag – what to do with the molasses syrup which remained. Early Spanish settlers noticed that the residual molasses was quick to ferment in the heat. However, it tasted terrible. So they experimented further making crude distillations which tasted better, and gradually, after trial and error, they made the product more refined and pleasant tasting. Freebooters took the new product to England and elsewhere.

Rum's growth in popularity

It was immediately popular in the British colonies and on the East Coast of America. Traded for pine logs and dried figs, it eventually became part of the slave trade when boats loaded with the spirit sailed to Africa and used it to barter for slaves. To combat scurvy and to act as a stimulant and general-purpose disinfectant, the Royal Navy issued rum rations to its fleet in 1655. Every man on board was entitled to a half pint of 80 per cent alcohol-strength rum.

Control of rum

But due to the many accidents on board, Admiral Sir Edward Vernon in 1740 commanded that henceforward the rum ration would be diluted with an equal part of water. The Admiral was known as 'Old Grog' because he always wore a shabby coat made of grogram, a gum-stiffened, coarse cloth made from silk and mohair. His 'three water rum' was very unpopular and it quickly became known as 'grog', a name that has survived to this day to describe a drink of spirit and water. In Australia and New Zealand the word 'grog' is now used in a general sense to describe any alcoholic drink. The regular rum ration to the Royal Navy was discontinued in 1970.

Making rum

Rum may be made from sugar cane juice, but it is more usually made from molasses. Fresh sugar cane is cut up and crushed between roller mills and the residual *bagasse* is crushed once more so that all juice is expressed. The juice is boiled, the water content evaporates leaving behind a sugar solution, very dark in colour. This is then clarified and the resulting thick, heavy syrup is pumped into centrifugal machines, which crystallise the sugar and separate it from the dark, thick liquid known as molasses. This may be evaporated further to obtain more sugar, but eventually the molasses will be fermented to form the base for rum or to make alcohol for industrial purposes.

Fermentation

Before fermentation, the molasses is diluted with water and mixed with 'dunder' – the residue left in the stills from a previous distillation. Some distilleries allow this mash to sour by itself, letting natural yeasts descend on to the surface. But generally most distillers use pure-culture yeasts, which they claim give a better-flavoured end product. Depending on the style of rum required, the mash will undergo either a slow or quick fermentation.

Slow fermentation

This process is associated with all the big, heavy rums such as the traditional rums from Jamaica and Martinique. The fermentation can last for up to 20 days, after which the liquid will have an alcoholic strength of about 7 per cent. It will now be put into pot stills and distilled twice before being aged in cask. The new rum will be rich in congenerics – higher esters, acids, flavour and bouquet agents – and will have an alcohol strength of 150° proof (86 per cent by volume).

Quick fermentation

This is associated with the lighter rums such as those made in Cuba and Puerto Rico. The fermentation lasts for two to three days, and a special yeast culture is used. The liquid is then taken to a patent still for distillation. The new rum will be clear and very light in body and will have very few congenerics remaining. However, it will have a high alcohol strength of 160° proof (91 per cent by volume).

Maturation

The big, dark rums are matured in oak casts for three years or more. Often they are taken from the Caribbean and the intense heat to spend their maturing period in the damp and cooler climates of Britain and France, where less evaporation will occur. Before being bottled, their strength will be reduced by additions of demineralised water. Some colour will have been taken naturally from the wood, but it may also be necessary to add some caramel to enhance colour. This will ensure the characteristic deep colour and it will also have some influence on the final flavour.

The light, white rums get little or no ageing in cask. Once made and reduced to potable strength, they are immediately drinkable.

Drinking rum

Rum may be drunk neat, or with ice, or with one of a number of mixers such as, cola, 7-up, lime juice or lemonade. It is much favoured as a cocktail ingredient and is especially good in cool punches or hot winter warmers.

Styles of Caribbean rum

Barbados

This is a semi-light style of rum produced by pot and patent stills. These golden rums have a sweetish, smoky, soft flavour. **Cockspur** and **Mount Gay** are prime examples.

Cuba

Cuban rums are light and delicate and similar in style to those produced in Puerto Rico. Their original and world-famous Bacardi is now made elsewhere. In 1960 the Bacardi distillery was taken over by Castro and the Cuban government. They tried to keep the Bacardi brand name, but the parent company contested this in a court of law and won. The rum made at the original plant in Santiago de Cuba is now called **Havana Club**.

Guyana

These rums are known as Demerara rums. They are named after the local Demerara river, which runs through the sugar plantations. Both pot and patent stills are used to make these rums, and quick fermentation methods give them a lightness which makes them ideal for blending with other rums. The light rums are usually drunk locally. The dark-brown rums come mostly to Britain where they are matured in London warehouses.

Haiti

These are French-influenced rums and, like brandy, they get two separate distillations in pot stills. The first distillation results in a spirit called clarin, which was often, in the past, used as part of voodoo ceremonies. The second distillation produces a heavy, full-flavoured rum, which is then aged in cask.

Jamaica

The general style of Jamaican rum is rich, dark, heavy flavoured and pungent. However, there are six distinct classifications of rum made on the island, ranging from light to very heavy. The lighter rums are mostly consumed locally; the heavier rums, known as **Wedderburn** and **Plummer** are mostly exported, much coming to Britain where they are aged and blended. Britain's damp climate – in contrast to the heat of the Caribbean – allows the spirit to mature more slowly and with less evaporation from the cask. Jamaica also exports heavy rum concentrates to Germany and Austria, where they are blended with neutral spirit and called **Rum Verschnitt** and **Inlander Rum** respectively.

Martinique

These rums are made principally from cane juice and are rich, dark and have an affinity with Jamaican rums of the Wedderburn style. They are sometimes known as **French Rhums**, and those destined for French consumption are matured and blended in France, usually in Bordeaux or Le Havre. The very best are known as **Grande Arôme**. The brand leader in France is **Negrita**, a product of the famous Dillon distillery – now owned by Bardinet of Bordeaux. They also produce a white rum called **Old Nick**. Perhaps the most favoured international brand is **Rhum St James**, which can be amber or white. Both of these are superb, and so is the rum punch of Martinique. If you order one they will place before you a slice of lime, a small bottle of syrup, a bottle of rum, some water in an earthenware jug and some ice. When you are expected to do the mixing, you must follow local advice and use 'one of sour, two of sweet, three of strong and four of weak'.

Puerto Rico

Puerto Rican rums are usually light in body and dry to the taste. There are two styles available, white label (very light bodied) and gold label (slightly less light). Puerto Rico is also the largest producer of rums in the world and the Destileria Bacardi has the largest capacity of all. The main export is to the United States with popular brands

Bacardi and **Ronrico** dominating the market. The rums are distilled in patent stills from a product known as blackstrap molasses. Special cultivated yeast is used during the fermentation process and strength reduction is achieved by additions of clear mountain water.

Trinidad

Trinidadian rums made by the patent-still method are mainly light to medium in character. They are well made, but lack real depth of flavour, which makes them more suited for mixing and blending.

—— Rums from other countries ——

United States

Rum was the first spirit to be distilled in North America. Blackstrap molasses was brought in from the West Indies to Connecticut, Rhode Island and Massachusetts, and distilled into full-bodied, strong, hearty rums. Some was kept for home consumption but most was traded abroad for goods not yet available in the New World. Rum trading became so popular that by 1750 there were more than 60 rum distilleries operating in Massachusetts alone.

An important part of the business became known as the 'Triangular Trade'. Rum was transported from New England by ship to Africa and traded for slaves. The slaves were then taken to the West Indies and traded for molasses, which was then brought back to New England and distilled into rum. Rum is rarely produced in the United States today. Popular commercial brands are all imported.

Australia

Sugar plantations were first founded in Queensland in the mid 1860s. The production of rum soon followed. The rum centre was established north of Brisbane in a town called Bundaberg in 1888. Made by a double distillation using the patent and pot-still method, the rum is aged for two years in huge American oak vats. The brand leader is **Bundaberg** or 'Bundy' for short and is of good quality.

Brazil

Rum in Brazil is called Aguardente de Cana or Cachaça. It is produced from a combination of molasses and cane juice and is mostly exported to the United States, South America and Japan. Popular brands are **Cana Rio**, **Dreher**, **Pirassununga**, Sâo Francisco and **Ypióca**.

South Africa

Rum became popular in South Africa in the 1950s and it now vies with the native brandy as the favoured spirit. **Mainstay**, their white, light brand has an international reputation for quality.

Venezuela

Venezuela is noted for one fine-quality rum – **Ron Añejo Pampero Especial**. The rum is cask-aged for two, three, sometimes four years.

Classic mixed drinks using rum as a base

Daiquiri

2 measures white rum
1 measure lime juice
½ teaspoon caster sugar
ice

Shake all the ingredients together. Strain into a cocktail glass. Decorate with lemon or orange peel.

Virgin's Prayer (serves 2)

2 measures light rum
2 measures dark rum
2 measures kahlúa (or other coffee-flavoured liqueur)
2 tablespoons lemon juice
4 tablespoons orange juice
ice

Shake all the ingredients together and strain into two highball glasses. Decorate each with a grape or strawberry.

Cuba Libre

1 measure white rum
Juice of ½ lime
cola
ice

Place rum with lime juice and ice in a highball glass. Add cola to taste. Decorate with slices of lime and lemon.

Pina Colada

2 measures white rum
2 measures pineapple juice
2 teaspoons coconut milk or coconut liqueur
2 dashes Angostura bitters
1 pinch salt
ice

Shake all the ingredients together. Pour into a highball glass. Decorate with pineapple, coconut and cherries.

Mai Tai

½ measure dark rum
1 measure light rum
½ measure tequila
½ measure curaçao or Cointreau
1 measure apricot brandy
1 measure orange juice
2 dashes grenadine
1 dash Angostura bitters
ice

Shake all the ingredients together. Put two ice cubes in a Paris goblet and strain in the cocktail. Decorate with pineapple and cherries.

Louisiana Lullaby

2 measures dark rum
4 teaspoons Dubonnet
1 teaspoon Grand Marnier
ice

Stir all the ingredients together with ice and strain into a cocktail glass. Decorate with a lemon slice.

Costa del Sol

2 measures white rum
1 measure sweet red vermouth
1 measure sugar syrup
½ measure fresh lemon juice
2½ measures soda water
ice

Add all the ingredients to a tall ice-filled glass. Decorate with a slice of orange and a cocktail cherry.

Banana Daiquiri

2 measures white rum
1 measure crème de banane
1 measure fresh orange juice
¼ measure fresh mashed banana
1 teaspoon caster sugar
1 teapsoon whipping cream
crushed ice

Put all the ingredients, except the ice in a blender. Blend well. Add a glassful of crushed ice. Blend again for a few seconds. Pour into a wine goblet. Decorate with slices of banana and pineapple, speared with a cherry.

La Paz

1 measure white rum
½ measure Italian red vermouth
½ measure Grand Marnier
1 teaspoon fresh lime juice
2 measures cold cola
broken ice

Add all the ingredients to a rocks glass half-filled with broken ice. Stir very gently. Decorate with a twist of lime.

Hollywood Nuts

1 measure white rum
½ measure Amaretto
½ measure crème de cacao
½ measure Frangelico
1 teaspoon egg white
1 measure 7up or lemonade
ice

Shake all the ingredients, except the 7up and strain into an ice-filled rocks glass. Add the 7up.

Columbus Cocktail

1½ measures golden rum
¾ measure apricot brandy
1 measure fresh lime juice
crushed ice

Shake the ingredients with crushed ice. Strain into a cocktail glass. Add a slice of lime.

Bacardi Cocktail

1½ measures Bacardi white rum
1 measure fresh lime juice
½ measure sugar syrup
1 teaspoon grenadine
ice

Shake all the ingredients with ice. Strain into a wine goblet. Decorate with a cherry.

Arrowhead

1 measure dark rum
½ measure Southern Comfort
½ measure crème de banane
¼ measure fresh lime juice
2½ measures lemonade
broken ice

Add all the ingredients to a rocks glass half-filled with broken ice. Stir very gently.

Rum Sunday

1 measure dark rum
½ measure sweet sherry
½ measure grenadine
3 tablespoons vanilla ice
2 teaspoons overproof dark rum
crushed ice

Blend all the ingredients except the strong rum briefly with a glassful of crushed ice. Pour into a tall glass. Float the strong rum on top. Sprinkle with grated chocolate.

Oyster Bay

1 measure dark rum
1 teaspoon anisette
2 measures mango juice
1 measure grapefruit juice
1 measure pineapple juice
1 measure papaya juice
¾ measure fresh lime juice
½ measure sugar syrup
ice

Shake all the ingredients together and strain into a tall ice-filled glass. Decorate with fruit. Serve with two straws.

Original Planters Punch

1⅜ measures Myers's dark rum
1 teaspoon grenadine
1 teaspoon caster sugar
juice of half a lime
4 measures fresh orange juice
ice

Shake all the ingredients together and strain into a tall glass filled with crushed ice. Decorate with a cherry and a slice of orange.

10
OTHER SPIRITS

Okolehao

This is a very popular Hawaiian spirit. It is first fermented from the juice of the baked roots of the sacred Ti plant (*cordyline australis*). The roots are rich in laevulose (fructose) and the juice ferments easily. After fermentation the spirit is distilled in a column or continuous still. After distillation the liquid is charcoal-filtered and immediately bottled; it gets no ageing. The spirit was first made by William Stevenson, an Australian, in 1790. It is marketed as crystal clear or golden. It is known locally as oke. It can be drunk neat or on the rocks or with mixers – coke and oke is a 'buzz' drink. It is also used in the preparation of some cocktails such as Scratch Me Lani and Mahalo which means 'thank you'.

Tiquira

Tiquira is a highly rectified, high-strength spirit made in Brazil. It is distilled from malted and fermented tapioca roots.

Poteen

Pronounced *potcheen*, and also known as Mountain Dew, poteen is an illicit style of whiskey made along the Irish Sea coast in mobile, miniature pot stills. It is Ireland's answer to American 'moonshine'. The spirit is usually made from potatoes and distilled in isolated mountain locations. Sometimes the distillation takes place on boats which are taken out on the ocean in order to dissipate any odour emanating from the stills. Much of the stuff tastes like firewater, but some is also fine – smooth, white and wonderful.

Schochu

This Japanese schnapps-style spirit is made from fermented sweet potato juice, which is distilled into a clear spirit.

11
LIQUEURS

Liqueurs are flavoured and sweetened spirits produced in a galaxy of beautiful and exciting colours. In America they are called cordials. Although liqueurs of a kind were made in Greek and Roman times, many of those we know today originated in the monasteries and abbeys of France and Italy.

Liqueurs were first made as medicines and general cure-alls to combat colds and fevers, but now they are taken mainly at the end of a meal for pleasure and to aid digestion. Undoubtedly, they have digestive qualities, especially those liqueurs compounded of herbs and seeds such as peppermint and caraway. Certainly they are pleasurable to drink. Their distinctive colours are a delight to the eye and their subtle aromas and exquisite flavours enhance the pleasures of good living.

Making liqueurs

All liqueurs are made from secret recipes, each formula a closely guarded secret. However, there are usually four definable elements in most liqueurs.

- basic spirit
- raw materials for flavouring
- sugar for sweetening
- colour when required.

Basic spirit

This consists of one of the following:

- neutral spirit
- brandy
- rum
- whisky
- fruit eau de vie
- rice spirit.

Raw materials

The raw materials elements can consist of:

- **Herbs**   Basil, cocoa leaves, herb ivy, hyssop, marjoram, peppermint, rosemary, sage, tarragon, tea leaves, thyme and wormwood.
- **Barks and woods**   Angostura, cinchona, cinnamon, myrrh, sandalwood and sassafras.
- **Drugs and roots**   Alant, angelica, calamus, celery, cloves, galanga, gentian, ginger, henna, liquorice, lovage, orris root, rhubarb, turmeric, valerian and zedoary.
- **Flowers**   Ivy, lavender, lily, rose petals, saffron and violets.
- **Seeds**   Allspice, angelica seeds, aniseed, cactus, cardamom, caraway, cumin, celery seeds, cocoa, coffee, coriander, dill, fennel, hazelnuts, mace, nutmeg, peppers, pimentoes and vanilla.
- **Fruit**   Apples, apricots, bananas, blackberries, blackcurrants, cherries, dates, grapefruit, lemons, mandarins, melons, oranges, passion fruit, peaches, pineapples, plums, raisins, raspberries and strawberries.
- **Dairy produce**   Cream, milk.

Sweetening

Beet sugar, sugar syrup or honey are the sweeteners used in liqueur recipes.

Colour

Although some liqueurs, for example fruit liqueurs, show their natural colours and others are marketed colourless, most are artificially coloured with natural vegetable matter for psychological and commercial reasons.

Flavours

Three methods are used to obtain the flavours: maceration, percolation or distillation.

Maceration

The maceration method is associated with the production of fruit liqueurs. The fruit is usually soft and fresh, but dried fruit is often added. The fruit is crushed before it is put into casks or vats which contain an appropriate quantity of brandy. The fruit is steeped in the brandy for six to nine months. The mix is stirred from time to time so that maximum colour, aroma and flavour are extracted from the fruit. Heating the mixture can speed up the operation, but experience shows that cold maceration gives the best results. The fruit-flavoured brandy is drawn off and filtered.

The mass of fruit remaining will also contain brandy and essential flavouring oils, and this is placed in a still where the remaining flavours and alcohol are extracted by distillation. This resulting extract is added to the flavoured brandy to give more character. If fruit stones were present in the original mash, some of their oils will also have been extracted which is why there is a hint of bitter almond in liqueurs made from apricots, cherries, peaches or plums.

The new liqueur is sweetened and kept in a maturing vat for another year where the air penetrating the pores of wood will mellow the blend and enhance and intensify the flavour and fragrance. Before being bottled the new liqueur will be given more filtrations and cold treatment to ensure the clarity and healthy appearance of the drink.

Percolation

The percolation method is usually associated with plants, leaves and herbs. The apparatus used has two levels – the bottom level holds the spirit and the upper level holds the flavouring agents. The operation works on the lines of a coffee percolator. The hot or cold spirit is pumped up over the flavourings and allowed to mingle and percolate through the flavourings, extracting flavours and aromas before being carried down into the bottom level. The pumping and percolation action is repeated continuously over weeks until all the flavours and essential oils have been extracted. The spirit-soaked flavourings are then distilled to extract any remaining flavours. This distillate is added to the percolate and the mixture is filtered and sent to be matured in vats for varying times. Before being bottled, it will be sweetened and mostly artificially coloured.

Distillation

The distillation is usually carried out in a medium-sized pot still which has a suspended basket tray to hold the flavouring agents known as botanicals – usually plants, seeds, herbs and roots. The botanicals are steeped in brandy for two days and the mash is placed on a tray in the still and brandy is added underneath. Heat is applied and the alcoholic vapours rise to permeate through the botanicals; the flavour-imbued vapours are condensed into a highly flavoured spirit. This is matured in oak casks for some time, where it will harmonise and mellow. It will be filtered, sweetened and probably artificially coloured before being bottled.

Types of liqueurs

The number of liqueurs made nowadays is legion. A modern phenomenon of the drinks industry is the emergence of cream liqueurs which have created worldwide interest. Baileys, the world's best-selling liqueur, was launched in Dublin in 1974. Its success has spawned a host of liqueurs of similar style, mostly emanating from Ireland. These include Carolans, Saint Brandan's, Feeneys, O'Gradys, Tara, O'Darby, Waterford, Ryan's, Sheridans, The Dubliner and Emmet's. Cream liqueurs should not be confused with the family of *crèmes* where the main flavour is predominant in the name such as crème de bananes, crème de cassis and crème de menthe.

Abricotine

This is a French liqueur is made at Enghien les Baines, near Paris, from apricots and their kernels which are macerated in brandy.

Advocaat

This is a popular Netherlands drink made from fresh egg yolks, grape brandy and sugar. It is thick and creamy and the flavour is sometimes enhanced by additions of orange, lemon, vanilla and kirsch. In Europe, rum-flavoured advocaat is also popular but chocolate and mocha-flavoured advocaats have only limited appeal. Perhaps the best way to enjoy advocaat is as a Snowball. Put two tablespoons of advocaat into a glass, top-up with fizzy lemonade.

Aiguebelle

Produced in a Trappist Abbey near Montélimar in France this liqueur is made from 50 different herbs, roots and plants grown in the Provence region. These are macerated in alcohol and then slowly distilled to extract the full flavour. After sweetening and maturing, the liqueur is coloured either green or yellow – the latter being the sweeter of the two.

Amaretto di Saronno

An almond and apricot-flavoured liqueur, this was first made commercially in the eighteenth century by the Reina family who ran an apothecary in Saronna, Italy. The original recipe was invented by a beautiful innkeeper in 1525. She had as a lodger Bernadino Luini, a painter from the Leonardo da Vinci school. Luini persuaded the innkeeper to be the model for the Madonna in his fresco of the nativity, which now hangs in the Sanctuary of Santa Maria della Grazie in Saronno. She was so proud and grateful she made the painter an original liqueur from the produce of her garden. She steeped the ingredients in alcohol and named the love potion Amaretto di Saronno.

Anisette

This is a strong aniseed-flavoured liqueur which has a pure spirit base. It ws made in 1750 by **Marie Brizard** in Bordeaux. It was then intended to be a medicine but it was later sweetened into a liqueur for commercial purposes. It is still made by the Brizard company. Other liqueurs of similar type are **Anis del Mono** from Spain, **Anisetta Stellata** (Italy), **Escarchado** (Portugal), and **Tres Castillos** (Puerto Rico).

Archers

Made from a combination of peaches and schnapps, this liqueur is crisp and clean-tasting on the palate.

Argentarium

A herb-flavoured liqueur, this is made by the Passionist Fathers in a huge monastery located 60 miles north of Rome.

Atholl Brose

This Scottish speciality was once described as 'a giant's drink'. Originally it was made from fine oatmeal, whisky, honey, herbs and cream. A modern prize-winning brand called **Dunkeld Atholl Brose** dispenses with the oatmeal and uses only 12-year-old malt whisky as the base ingredient. It is now described as 'a whisky liqueur of rare distinction'.

Aurum

This golden, predominantly orange-flavoured liqueur, is made at Pescara, Italy. The special oranges and herbs are harvested in the Abruzzi mountains and macerated in 10-year-old brandy before being matured in oak casks.

Baerenfang

A German liqueur with a neutral spirit base this is flavoured with lime and mullein flowers. Another lime-flavoured liqueur is **Crema de Lima** from Spain.

Bahia

This bitter-sweet Brazilian liqueur is coffee flavoured and has a base of grain spirit which is made locally.

Baileys Irish Cream

Currently the world's best-selling liqueur, it was launched by Gilbeys,

Dublin, in 1974. It combines Irish whiskey and Irish cream together with vanilla and cocoa extracts. During early experimentation the difficulty was to prevent the cream from curdling and separating from the other ingredients. The problems were resolved by a special homogenisation method that breaks up the cream's fat into tiny molecules that bind the ingredients together. Only absolutely fresh Irish dairy cream is used, with a butterfat content of 48 per cent – twice that of household cream. The whiskey used is three years old, triple distilled, and mellowed in American oak casks.

Bénédictine

This is one of the great classic liqueurs. It was first made in 1510 at the Bénédictine monastery at Fécamp in Normandy, France, by Dom Bernardo Vincelli. It was initially made as a medicine and even today some people take it to soothe stiff limbs and to ease the pain of rheumatism. Bénédictine is made from double-distilled Cognac brandy and 75 different herbs and plants, and is aged for four years before bottling. When Francis I of France visited the monastery in 1534 he was enchanted with the drink which was then called 'Bénédictine ad Majorem Dei Gloriam' – Bénédictine for the greater glory of God. During the French Revolution the monastery was destroyed and for the next 70 years there was no Bénédictine made. In 1863 a scholar called Alexandre Le Grand unearthed the recipe – previously thought to have been destroyed – and he set about relaunching the liqueur on a secular and commercial basis. The liqueur is no longer produced by the religious order, but each bottle label acknowledges the religious connections with the initials DOM – *Deo Optimo Maximo*, meaning to 'God, most good, most great'. Bénédictine is rather sweet, and some years ago the directors of the distillery decided to add another drier-style liqueur to their list. They blended Bénédictine and brandy together and named it **B&B**.

Brontë

A Yorkshire liqueur, named after the literary Brontë sisters, it has a base of French brandy and added flavour comes from oranges, herbs, honey and spices.

Cassis

This is a liqueur particularly associated with Dijon in Burgundy, France. Liqueur de cassis is made by macerating destalked black-currants in brandy or fruit eau de vie. It is strong flavoured, sweet and red, and is more properly called crème de cassis. It is popular on its own or mixed with the dry, white wine Bourgogne Aligoté (as Kir) or with Champagne (as Kir Royale). It is also used to flavour ices and fruits including fruit salads. It should not be confused with sirop de cassis which is non-alcoholic.

Cerasella

A deep red liqueur, this is made from cherries and a variety of mountain herbs collected in the vicinity of Abruzzi in Italy. It is one of Italy's most popular liqueurs and it was supposed to be a favourite of the legendary d'Annunzio, the Italian poet and thinker.

The final stages of liqueur production

CRÊMES

Crême means 'cream', which originally meant that the drink had been sweetened. In contemporary usage it means that the specified liqueur tastes exclusively of the flavouring name or that it has one distinct flavour predominating. There are numerous crême liqueurs on the market, but three in particular have international reputations for quality – crême de cacao, crême de menthe and crême Yvette.

Crême de Cacao

Chocolate is a popular flavouring in many liqueurs. This liqueur is made either by maceration or percolation of cacao beans and is later distilled and sweetened. The original beans came from the Chouao Valley near Caracas, Venezuela. Now 'Chouao' when seen on the label, is a generic term for cacao beans produced anywhere in Venezuela.

The liqueur may be white or brown in colour and is especially good when used in combination with ice cream as a dessert.

Crême de Menthe

Almost every liqueur house makes a mint-flavoured liqueur. Crême de menthe is one of the best and best-known of all liqueurs. It used to be made only in France using the finest mint grown in England and fine-quality Cognac brandy. Now it is made in many countries, coloured white or dark, bright green. The best-known green style is the excellent Freezomint made by Cusenier in France.

Crême Yvette

This is a sweet and highly-scented American liqueur made in Philadelphia. It is made from the petals of the Parma violet and named in honour of the famous French actress and *diseuse* Yvette Guilbert who was at the peak of her fame in the 1890s.

Other crême liqueurs

Liqueur	Flavouring
crême d'ananas	pineapple
crême d'amandes	almond
crême de banane	banana
crême de café	coffee
crême de chocolat	cocoa
crême de ciel	orange
crême de cumin	caraway seed
crême de fraise	strawberry
crême de fraise de bois	wild strawberry
crême de framboise	raspberry
crême de guignolet	cherry
crême de kobai	plum
crême de mandarine	tangerine
crême de mokka	coffee
crême de myrtilles	bilberry
crême de noisette	hazelnut
crême de noix	walnut
crême de nuits	blackcurrant
crême de poire	pear
crême de prune	plum
crême de prunelle	sloe
crême de roses	rose
crême de vanille	vanilla
crême de violette	violet

These liqueurs are especially good when served frappé (with crushed ice).

Chartreuse

In 1605 the Carthusian monks were given a crude recipe by Maracel d'Estrées for the making of chartreuse. By 1764 the monks had perfected the recipe but the liqueur remained unknown outside their monastery, located at Voiron, near Grenoble, France. In 1848 some army officers were quartered there and at the end of dinner they were offered the liqueur as a digestif. They were greatly impressed and the liqueur's reputation spread so quickly than in 1860 the monks built a new distillery at Fourvoirie to cope with the demand. The Carthusians were expelled from France in 1903 and they took the formula with them to Spain where they sought sanctuary. They settled in Tarragona and continued to make the liqueur. Their exile lasted until 1931 when the French government allowed them to resume making their liqueur near Grenoble. Today the liqueur is made by the Carthusian monks both in Tarragona and Voiron. It is made from a most complicated recipe which uses up to 135 different ingredients and a base of brandy. Green chartreuse, coloured with chlorophyll, is the original formula with a strong alcohol content of 55 per cent. Yellow chartreuse, coloured with saffron, is a much sweeter variation with a strength of 43 per cent alcohol.

Cherry brandy and cherry Heering

As their names suggest, these are cherry-flavoured liqueurs with a brandy base. They are very popular, especially in Europe where this style of liqueur is made in many countries including Denmark, Germany, France and Switzerland. Cherry Heering was invented by Peter Heering in Copenhagen more than 150 years ago. These styles should not be confused with true cherry brandies, such as kirsch which is distilled from the fermented juice of cherries.

Cocoribe

This is an American liqueur flavoured with Wild Island coconuts and Virgin Island rum.

Cointreau

The House of Cointreau was established in 1849 in Angers, France. Originally the liqueur, created by two confectioners, Edouard and

Adolphe Cointreau, was called Triple Sec but the style of liqueur became so imitated that it was changed to the family name of Cointreau. This white liqueur is a subtle harmony of natural white spirits, Mediterranean oranges and bitter West Indian oranges. It is at its most refreshing when served on the rocks.

Columba Cream

This is a Scottish blend of single malt whiskies, cream and honey.

Cordial Médoc

This sweet, red and brown, highly aromatic liqueur from Bordeaux is a blend of brandy, old claret, herb extracts, orange curaçao and crème de cacao – a cocktail of flavours that combine surprisingly well. The name cordial comes from the Latin word *cor* meaning 'of the heart', and it is taken to mean a stimulant or reviver.

Cuarenta y Tres

Popular Spanish liqueur made, as the name suggests, from 43 different ingredients – mainly herbs – but with discernible tones of banana and vanilla in the flavour. Also known as **Licor 43**, it is produced in Cartagena.

Curaçao

The bitter oranges which originally flavoured this famous liqueur came from the island of Caraçao off the coast of Venezuela. Nowadays the oranges come from many sources and the liqueur from many countries, but principally from France and the Netherlands. Curaçao is produced in a variety of colours including white, orange, blue, green and brown. It used to be known as Triple Sec, as did Cointreau – not a very apt name for sweet liqueurs.

Danzig Goldwasser

This was originally produced in Poland by the firm of Der Lacks in 1598. After war destruction, the business moved to Berlin where the liqueur is still made using the original recipe. This water-white, sweet liqueur is flavoured with aniseed, caraway and herbs, and each bottle contains tiny specks of gold leaf. The combination is believed to speed recuperation, aid digestion and act as a general tonic. The much less poular **Danzig Silberwasser** has silver flakes instead of gold.

Drambuie

Translated from the Gaelic, *An dram buidheach* means 'the drink that satisfies'. It is the classic Scottish liqueur formerly made in the Isle of Skye but now made in the Lothians. The original recipe was formulated by Prince Charles Edward Stuart, popularly known as Bonnie Prince Charlie. When his army was defeated by the Hanoverian army at the Battle of Culloden in 1746, the Prince fled for his life to the Isle of Skye with Captain John MacKinnon, one of his supporters and a native of Skye. MacKinnon managed to get the Prince on to a ship bound for France and the Prince, in gratitude, gave MacKinnon his secret recipe for making his personal liqueur. The liqueur is still made by the MacKinnon family, combining fine, aged malt whisky with herbs, spices and heather honey.

Fior d'Alpi

The name literally means 'flower of the Alps'. A particularly good style is **Mille Fiori**. As the name suggests, the flavour is extracted from a thousand flowers, along with herbs gathered in the Italian Alps. The liqueur is sold in tall, narrow, clear bottles containing a sugar-encrusted twig reminiscent of a Christmas tree. Two other Italian liqueurs **Edelweiss** and **Isolabella** are somewhat similar.

Forbidden Fruit

This is an American liqueur made from a large citrus fruit called shaddock, which resembles a grapefruit and has a bitter-sweet character. Oranges are added and the fruits are macerated in fine brandy and later sweetened with honey. The liqueur was considered to be so unique it was dubbed 'Nectar of the Gods' – forbidden to humans.

Frangelico

This is an Italian liqueur made from an infusion of wild hazelnuts, berries, herbs and flowers.

Galliano

This distinctive, pale yellow, herb liqueur from Italy was first made in 1896 by Armando Vaccari as a tribute to Major Giuseppe Galliano. During the Italian–Abyssinian war (1895–6) the major held the fort of Enda Jesus for 44 days until he was ordered to surrender. The liqueur was first made in Livorno, Tuscany, but it is now made in a modern liqueur plant at Salara near Milan. The fort of Enda Jesus is always depicted on the label of the tall, elegant, Galliano bottles. The liqueur is made from a blend of more than 30 herbs and a variety of flowers, berries and roots. Some vanilla and anise is also added, and the ingredients are infused and distilled in fine spirit. The new liqueur is rested and the flavours allowed to harmonise in glass tanks for up to six months before being filtered and bottled.

Galliano has become very well known due principally to the cocktail Harvey Wallbanger. Harvey was a skilled surfer in California. One day, after losing an important competition, he consoled himself with his favourite drink, a Screwdriver (vodka and orange juice) with a splash of Galliano. He had a few too many, and when he eventually left the bar he bounced from wall to wall. He and his drink became known as Harvey Wallbanger.

Gallways Irish Coffee Liqueur

This is a rich, smokey, smooth liqueur with a most definite flavour of coffee. It has a base of mature Irish whiskey with herbs and honey also included in the dark-brown blend.

Glayva

The name of this liqueur means 'very good' in Gaelic. It is made from a combination of old Scotch whisky, herbs, spices, aromatic oil and honey.

Glen Mist

Because of the shortage of raw materials in Britain at the time, this Scottish liqueur was made in Ireland from 1945 until 1963 when it returned home. While it was made in Ireland it had an Irish whiskey base, but it has since reverted to its original recipe of high-quality, fully matured Scotch whisky flavoured with herbs, honey and spices.

Grand Marnier

This is one of the great orange-flavoured liqueurs. The Grand Marnier Company was launched by the Lapostolle family in 1827 in a small village located between Lyon and Grenoble in France. They experimented with the blending of bitter oranges from Haiti with Cognac brandy and, finally, in 1880 Grand Marnier was launched. Today the liqueur is partly made in Cognac and partly in Paris. It is now flavoured with the juice of wild Caribbean oranges, orange peel and aromatics. The flavouring agents are macerated in Cognac and then distilled. The distillation is then blended with old Cognac and sugar syrup. It is rested to allow the flavours to marry before being filtered and bottled. The standard style is **Cordon Rouge** which has 40 per cent alcohol by volume. The other quality is **Cordon Jaune** which is of a lower strength. Grand Marnier is delicious as a liqueur, but it is also an important culinary ingredient for dishes such as Soufflé Grand Marnier, Crêpes Suzette and Canard à l'Orange.

Heather Cream

A smooth blend of malt whisky and cream, this is produced on the outskirts of Airdrie, Scotland.

Irish Mist

Ireland's answer to Drambuie! It was first made at the time when the manufacture of the Scottish liqueur Glen Mist was transferred to Tullamore in Ireland. It has an Irish whiskey base and is flavoured with exotic herbs and clover and heather honey.

Irish Velvet

This is a mixture of Jameson's Irish whiskey, coffee and sugar. It may be drunk as it is, or add hot water and float double cream on top for an Irish Coffee.

Izarra

The liqueur comes from the Basque region of south-west France. The word translated means 'star' because the liqueur is considered to have star quality. It is made with a base of Armagnac brandy and flavoured with fruits, honey and flowers from the French Pyrenees. It is compounded in two qualities – yellow which has an alcohol strength of 43 per cent and the stronger, more intensely flavoured green, which has 55 per cent alcohol. It was first introduced in 1835.

Kahlúa

This is one of the world's biggest-selling liqueurs. It is an exotic blend of cane spirit, coffee and vanilla. Mexican in origin, it is also made under licence by the Heering family in Denmark. It is drunk on its own or frappé (one part kahlúa to four parts milk with plenty of crushed ice), or enjoyed supremely when poured over ice cream to make a dessert of instant perfection.

Kirsch

The water-white liqueur is made in Alsace and in Germany from a distillation of cherries and their kernels. An outstanding example is **Schwarzwald Kirschwasser** from Germany's Black Forest region.

Krupnik

This is an increasingly popular Polish liqueur. It is prepared from an ancient recipe using honey, various juices and aromatic herbs.

Kümmel

Although it originated in Eastern Europe, it is now made in many countries, especially Germany. It has a neutral spirit base and the flavour comes from caraway seeds, cumin, orris root and fennel. It is considered to be one of the very best digestifs because of the choice of the ingredients used.

Kumquat

This orange-flavoured liqueur is made, as its name suggests, from kumquats, which are oval-shaped citrus fruits. It is a speciality of Corfu, Greece.

Le Touché

The liqueur is produced in Armagnac from oranges and herbs which are macerated in aged Armagnac brandy and then sweetened with sugar syrup. In France, a small measure of the liqueur is often added to dry, chilled, sparkling wine such as Blanquette de Limoux, and this combination makes a wonderful, refreshing apéritif called Mousquetaire.

Malibu

This is a fairly recent introduction to the family of liqueurs. It is made from the finest Caribbean white rum and flavoured with tropical coconut. It is sometimes used as a prime ingredient for exotic cocktails and long drinks.

Mandarin Napoléon

This Belgian tangerine and Cognac brandy-flavoured liqueur was first introduced in 1892. The peel of fresh tangerines, steeped in brandy, is distilled with the essential oils of the fruit. The distillate is blended with Napoléon brandy. It is then rested for some time to allow the flavours to marry. After filtration this elegant liqueur is bottled for sale.

Maraschino

Originally from Dalmatia in the former Yugoslavia, it was first made in 1779 and is now made by many liqueur producers in Italy. It gets its pleasing flavour from bitter Marasca cherries and their crushed kernels and almonds. Sugar syrup is added to give a sweet sensation on the palate. Maraschino is often used to embellish fruit salads and dishes with a predominantly cherry flavour.

Midori

This green-coloured, Japanese liqueur was created by Suntory in 1978. It is made from the native musk melon and is sweet, sticky – almost crystalline – with melon and apple overtones in the flavour. *Midori* is Japanese for 'green'.

Parfait Amour

Perfect Love is the translated name, but not everyone loves this liqueur. To some palates it can taste sickly sweet. It is flavoured with oil of violets, rose petals, vanilla, almonds, citrus fruits, coriander and sugar. Aimed at romantics it is coloured purple to imply passion.

Royal Mint Chocolate

This was first introduced in 1960 by its creator Dr Peter Hallgarten. It has a predominantly, creamy, chocolate and peppermint flavour. It is one of the 'Royal family' of liqueurs which this specialist has produced. Others include **Royal Cherry Chocolate**, **Royal Coconut Chocolate**, **Royal Fruit and Nut Chocolate**, **Royal French Coffee-Chocolate**, **Royal Apricot Chocolate** and the **Royal Jubilee Liqueur**.

Sabra

This Israeli chocolate-orange liqueur was introduced in the 1960s. It is made from the sabra cactus which grows well in hardy desert land and is blended with jaffa oranges and chocolate. Rehovot is the centre of production. Another Israeli orange-flavoured liqueur is **Hallelujah**.

Sambuca

This water-white liqueur is one of the most favoured of Italian liqueurs. It is flavoured with elderberry and liquorice. When served in restaurants, three – and only three – coffee beans are floated on top of the liqueur in the glass. The liqueur is then flamed and the heat extracts flavour from the beans.

Sheridans

This is a unique, twin-part, Irish whiskey-based liqueur, made in Dublin. It is formulated to have a rich, dark body and a smooth, creamy head when poured into a glass. The liqueur is presented in an attractive, split-chamber, glass bottle that holds the black spirit side by side with the white, ready for layering into the glass. The black, lower layer is chocolate and coffee flavoured, the upper layer tastes of cream and vanilla. Uniform pouring is made possible by a novel and ingenious one-cap, 'perfect pour' spout.

Southern Comfort

Originally an American liqueur, it is also made under licence in some other countries. Traditionally it had a bourbon whiskey base but today it can have a neutral spirit base and up to 100 flavouring ingredients. Prominent among these are peaches and oranges. It is a very big seller worldwide.

Stag's Breath

A blend of Speyside whisky and fermented comb honey, this liqueur takes its name from one of the whiskies mentioned in Sir Compton Mackenzie's book *Whisky Galore*.

Strega

A bright-yellow liqueur made from more than 70 different herbs, fruits and barks in Benevento, Naples. Legend has it the liqueur was first made by witches disguised as beautiful maidens. The name actually means 'witch' in Italian and locals say that those who share Strega will remain good friends.

Tia Maria

The original coffee-flavoured liqueur. It is made in Jamaica using five-year-old native rum as a base and the distinctive Blue Mountain coffee as its main flavour. In restaurants it is usually served with cream floating on top.

Van der Hum

A South African liqueur made from a combination of mature native brandy, naartjies (a local variety of tangerine), spices and herbs, this pale yellow, fresh-tasting liqueur was evolved by accident. Dutch colonists of the Cape tried to recreate their homeland favourite Cointreau using local ingredients. They failed, but were delighted with the result and called it Van der Hum. The name roughly translated from the Afrikaans means 'what's-his-name'. A favourite local drink is Brandy Hum which is a combination of the liqueur and brandy.

Vieille Cure

The name literally means 'old rectory' which refers to the origins of the liqueur at the Abbaye de Cenon in the Gironde, Bordeaux. This fairly dry, herb-flavoured liqueur, originally intended to be used as a medicine, has a base of Cognac and Armagnac brandies.

Drinking liqueurs

Liqueurs are considered to be natural digestifs, and for that reason they are recognised as after-dinner drinks. They are also important ingredients for some cocktails and mixed drinks. In addition, they are used in the kitchen for baking and for flavouring sorbets, ice creams, fruit dishes and puddings. On their own they are usually taken neat. Some, like Tia Maria, are served with cream floating on top, others like crême de menthe are served frappé (with crushed ice.) Cream liqueurs such as Baileys are normally served chilled or on the rocks (with ice cubes). Liqueurs are sometimes served as cooling, long drinks using mixers such as soda water, lemonade, tonic and ice. A feature and a virtue of liqueurs is that they remain in good condition long after the bottle is breached.

Classic mixed drinks using liqueurs as a base

Grasshopper

½ measure crême de menthe
½ measure white crême de cacao
½ measure cream
ice

Shake all the ingredients together with ice and strain into a champagne glass.

Widow's Kiss

½ measure Bénédictine
½ measure chartreuse
1 measure Calvados
1 dash Angostura bitters
ice

Shake all the ingredients together and strain into a cocktail glass. Decorate with a slice of strawberry and a slice of apple.

Honeymoon

1 measure Bénédictine
1 measure Calvados
juice of half an orange
ice

Shake all the ingredients together and strain into a cocktail glass. Decorate with a slice of orange and a slice of apple.

Shooters

1 measure Grand Marnier
¾ measure kahlúa
½ measure Baileys Irish Cream
ice

Shake with ice and strain into a cocktail glass.

Iceberg

1 measure Galliano
½ measure Cointreau
1 tablespoon orange-flavoured water ice
Mix in a blender. Serve in a stemmed glass. A straw is optional.

Pousse-Café or Rainbow Cocktail

This is spectaular combination of seven different ingredients which are poured over the back of a teaspoon into a liqueur glass, according to their specific gravity. The sequence of pouring is vital as the lighter product must always float on the denser to give a rainbow effect of different, clearly defined colours. You need a good eye to divide the drink into seven equal fractions and a steady hand to ensure that the ingredients do not mix as you pour. Below are two recipes for the rainbow cocktail which should be poured in ascending order.

Recipe A		Recipe B
½ crême de cacao	1	½ grenadine
½ crême de violette	2	½ crême de cacao
½ yellow chartreuse	3	½ Maraschino
½ Maraschino	4	½ orange Curaçao
½ Bénédictine	5	½ green crême de menthe
½ green chartreuse	6	½ Parfait Amour
½ Cognac brandy	7	½ Cognac brandy

Scarlett O'Hara

2 measures Southern Comfort
1 measure cranberry juice
⅛ measure fresh lime juice
ice

Put the ingredients into a shaker. Shake with ice and strain into a wine goblet filled with crushed ice. Decorate with a cherry on a stick. Serve with two straws.

She's Paying

1 measure kahlúa
½ measure Grand Marnier
1 teaspoon amaretto
1 measure vodka
ice

Shake all the ingredients together. Strain into rocks glass filled with crushed ice. Decorate with a cherry on a stick.

Black Dublinski

1 measure Baileys Irish Cream
1 measure kahlúa
1 measure vodka
½ measure dry sherry
ice

Put the ingredients into a shaker. Shake with ice. Strain into a wine goblet.

747

1 measure crême de cacao
1 measure Galliano
1 measure bourbon whiskey
1 measure vodka
1 measure single cream
crushed ice

Put all the ingredients into a blender. Blend to a smoothness. Serve in a tall glass.

Ah!

1 measure Tia Maria
1 measure Cointreau
1 measure Baileys Irish Cream
½ measure amaretto
ice
3 chocolate-covered coffee beans

Put the coffee beans in the bottom of a champagne flute glass. Add three lumps of ice. Pour the rest of the ingredients into a shaker. Shake vigorously with ice. Strain into the glass.

Rusty Nail

1 measure Drambuie
1 measure Scotch whisky
ice

Fill an old-fashioned glass with ice cubes. Pour in the Drambuie and whisky. Stir.

Prince Charlie

1 measure Drambuie
1 measure brandy
1 measure lemon juice
cracked ice

Shake vigorously with cracked ice. Strain into a cocktail glass.

Russian Bear

1 measure dark crème de cacao
1 measure vodka
1 tablespoon fresh, heavy cream
ice

Put some ice cubes into an old-fashioned glass. Pour in the other ingredients. Stir well.

Red Robin

1 measure white crême de cacao
1 measure vodka
1 measure cranberry juice
ice

Shake all the ingredients well with ice cubes. Strain into a cocktail glass.

Melancholy

2 measures crême de banane
1 measure golden rum
1½ measures crême de framboise
2½ measures pinapple juice
crushed ice

Blend all the ingredients with crushed ice until slushy. Serve in a cocktail glass. Decorate with a slice of lime.

Après Ski

1 measure white crême de cacao
1 measure peppermint schnapps
1 measure coffee liqueur
ice

Shake all the ingredients together with ice cubes. Strain into a cocktail glass filled with crushed ice.

Coconut Hug

1 measure crême de noyaux
½ measure apricot brandy
1 measure rum cream
2 measures cream of coconut
crushed ice

Put all the ingredients, including the crushed ice, into a blender. Blend and strain into a tall glass. Decorate with a maraschino cherry.

True Blue

1 measure blue curaçao
1 measure light rum
1 measure lemon juice
½ teaspoon caster sugar
crushed ice

Mix all the ingredients, including the crushed ice, together in a blender. Strain into a tall glass. Decorate with a sprig of mint and a wedge of pineapple.

Friar Tuck

2 measures frangelico
2 measures lemon juice
1 teaspoon grenadine
ice

Put ice cubes into a shaker. Add all the ingredients. Shake well. Strain into an old-fashioned glass. Decorate with a slice of orange and a maraschino cherry.

Abbot

1½ measures frangelico
2 measures unsweetened pineapple juice
¼ banana sliced
2 dashes orange bitters
crushed ice

Put all the ingredients including the crushed ice into a blender. Blend until smooth. Pour into a tumbler. Decorate with crushed hazlenuts.

Café Grand

1½ measures Grand Marnier
4 measures piping-hot coffee
1 sugar cube

Pour the coffee into a heat-proof glass. Put the sugar cube on a teaspoon and sprinkle it with one teaspoon Grand Marnier. Rest the teaspoon on the rim of the glass and ignite the sugar cube. Allow it to burn for a few seconds. Lower the sugar cube into the coffee. Add the remaining Grand Marnier. Stir gently.

12
AFTERS

Coffees flavoured with spirits and liqueurs

An excellent way to enjoy spirits and liqueurs is to add them to coffee and cream. The original spirit-flavoured coffee was invented by an Irish head chef, Willy Ryan, who worked at Shannon Airport in the south-west of Ireland, in the days when transatlantic aeroplanes stopped at Shannon to refuel. To combat the cold, damp weather the chef would offer the weary travellers his special concoction which he called Gaelic Coffee. This warming, comforting and delicious drink soon became an international favourite, and the saviour of the Irish whiskey industry as well.

How to make Gaelic Coffee

The original recipe for Gaelic Coffee, known also as Irish Coffee, is as follows:

    1 measure Irish whiskey
    2 teaspoons brown sugar
    150 ml (5 fl. oz) scalding-hot, strong black coffee
    double cream

Into a 250 ml (8 oz) stemmed goblet place the whiskey and sugar – leave the teaspoon in the glass to conduct the heat and prevent the glass from cracking as you now pour in the piping-hot coffee. Stir the ingredients thoroughly because the sugar must be completely

dissolved. Sugar is important, not only for sweetening the drink, but as an aid to the successful floating of the cream. Remove the spoon and wait a few seconds for the surface to calm. Now, over the back of the same spoon, slowly pour the double cream, so that it floats on the surface of the coffee to form an attractive white collar 19 mm (¾ inch) thick. For complete enjoyment drink the whiskey-flavoured coffee through the cream.

Many countries have adapted this recipe to incorporate their native spirits and liqueurs to make their own specialities. The following is a selective list of the more established speciality coffees.

Coffee	Spirit or liqueur used
Calypso Coffee	Tia Maria
Caribbean Coffee	rum
Dutch Coffee	Genever
French Coffee (Café Royal)	Cognac
German Coffee	kirsch
Highland Coffee	Scotch whisky
Italian Coffee	Strega
Mexican Coffee	tequila or kahlúa
Monks' Coffee	Bénédictine
Normandy Coffee	Calvados
Russian Coffee	Vodka
Scandinavian Coffee	aquavit
Spanish Coffee	Fundador or any other Spanish brandy
Welsh Coffee	Can-y-Delyn or Prince of Wales

13

MIXING THEM
AT HOME

It is not difficult to mix drinks at home and achieve perfect results. Besides the ingredients required for the recipes all you need is some specialised equipment to allow you to do the best possible job and some appropriate glasses to display your creations to their best advantage. Equipment can be a problem but if you look around your kitchen you will probably find that you have all the items required with perhaps just a few exceptions.

—————— Equipment list ——————

Check with the following equipment list:

- **Ice-cube trays** for making ice.
- **Container** for holding ice – a glass jug will do but spray the ice with soda water to prevent the cubes from sticking together.
- **Ice tongs** to pick up the cubes, but a perforated spoon will also work – the object is to get the ice in the drink without any added water.
- **Ice crusher**, if you do not have one just wrap the ice cubes in a clean napkin and crush them with a hard object such as a kitchen mallet or rolling pin.
- **Glass jug with an involuted pourer** which holds back the ice. This jug is also useful for summer drinks such as fruit cups, wine cups and sangria. It can also substitute for a mixing glass and has the advantage of having an inbuilt strainer.

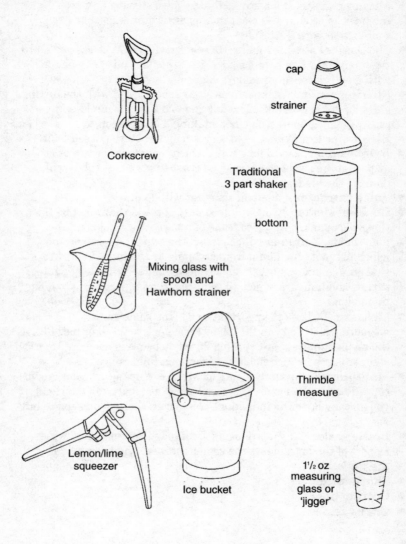

Corkscrew

cap

strainer

Traditional
3 part shaker

bottom

Mixing glass with
spoon and
Hawthorn strainer

Thimble
measure

Lemon/lime
squeezer

Ice bucket

1½ oz
measuring
glass or
'jigger'

Equipment for making your own mixed drinks

- **Mixing glass** used for drinks that require stirring and are intended to be thin and clear in appearance. It is used in conjunction with a strainer.
- The classical **strainer** is the Hawthorn which can be clipped on to the mixing glass to hold back the ice. It is flat and spoon-shaped with a spring coiled around its edges.
- **Stirring spoon**, also known as a bar spoon. Used with the mixing glass for stirring drinks. The flat end is used as a 'muddler' to crush sugar and mint, as when making a Mint Julep.
- **Blender** or **liquidiser**, used when drinks require puréed fruit.
- **Drinks mixer**, useful for drinks which include ice cream or cream as part of the recipe. Always used crushed ice as ice cubes will damage the blades.
- **Juice extractor** – a lemon squeezer will do fine.
- **Cocktail shaker** – you will need only one and that must be the three-part shaker which consists of a base which holds all the ingredients, a strainer which sits on the base and a cap on top which prevents the liquid from escaping as the ingredients are shaken. A shaker is necessary for ingredients such as egg whites, syrups and liqueurs which all require a thorough rousing to make them blend.
- **Measure** – it is most important to use the same sized measure which you can fill full or three-quarters full or half full, as the recipe requires. In Britain a 25 ml measure is used; in America a jigger is used which holds 1½ American fluid ounces.
- **Multipurpose opener**, a gadget which can open corked or crown-capped bottles and cans, it is also known as a bartender's friend. If you already have the individual accessories there is no need to buy one.
- **Bottle sealer** – if you are using Champagne or sparkling wines as part of the ingredients the sealer can save what remains in the bottle.
- **Sharp knife**
- **Cutting board**
- **Citrus zester**

Tricks of the trade

- Use the best possible ingredients.
- Always keep to the recipe. Try not to substitute ingredients.
- When using ice it should be clean and clear.
- Shaking – put plenty of ice in the shaker as this helps to chill the ingredients. Using plenty of ice also helps to contribute to a more rhythmic shaking action. When shaking use a short, snappy action. Prolonged shaking merely melts the ice and dilutes the drink.
- Use the right glass

(i) Champagne (ii) Paris goblet (iii) Rocks/Old fashioned (iv) Highball/Collins
(v) Cocktail (vi) Brandy (vii) Liqueur

- Stirring – when stirring mixed drinks, again use plenty of ice for fast chilling. The stirring action should be vigorous and continuous but just sufficient to get the drink well chilled.
- It is a good idea to serve the drinks in glasses which have been chilled in the fridge as this will help to keep the drink cooler, longer.
- Mixed drinks must be served immediately they are made – when they are in their peak condition. If drinks are left hanging around, the ingredients will soon separate.
- Do not fill glasses to the brim or over-decorate.

Glasses

Glasses should be clear, not coloured, and must be absolutely clean.

Frosting glasses

Some drinks require to be served in frosted glasses. You can easily frost the glass by dipping the rim in egg white and then immediately into caster sugar. You must allow the frosting to dry before using the glass. If the thought of egg white puts you off, simply cut an orange or lemon in half and wipe it over the rim of the glass and dip the glass rim into the sugar. Coloured sugar, if required, is easy to make by adding a few drops of food colouring to the sugar. You must blend in the colour well using a fork.

14

CULINARY USES OF SPIRITS AND LIQUEURS

Food and wine have long been accepted as natural partners, whether the wine is used to add flavour to the food or to accompany it. But the use of spirits and liqueurs in the kitchen is generally thought to be a luxury. Of course, we all accept that spirits and liqueurs are comparatively expensive, but given the small amounts that are required to add a rich, aromatic subtlety to a dish and to enhance the flavours of the other ingredients, it could be considered a false economy not to use them. Some people may be concerned about the alcohol content of these drinks, but when you add them to cooking liquids or when heat is applied to them, the alcohol soon evaporates and all you are left with are their enriching, mellow flavours. But what you must try to avoid is having too generous a hand in their use, as too much of the spirit or liqueur will drown the flavours of the other ingredients. Good chefs know from experience that the quality of the food can never rise above the quality of the ingredients, and that encompasses using good-quality liquors, as well.

Applications in cookery

Spirits

Brandy

Brandy is very versatile. It can be used to flavour soups (bisques), fish (especially shellfish), all kinds of meat, fruit (especially peaches), fruit cake and Christmas pudding, and trifles.

Calvados

Calvados goes very well with all apple dishes including stewed apple, apple crêpes, baked apple and apple charlotte. It also adds a lovely, subtle flavour to pork, chicken and veal. A Normandy dessert treat is to pour chilled Calvados over lime-flavoured ice cream.

Eaux de vie

These are wonderful when used to marinade their own basic fruits – kirsch with cherries, slivovitz with plums, Poire Williams with pears, framboise with crushed raspberries, fraise with strawberries, and so on. Add a dollop of vanilla ice cream for a delicious dessert. Eaux de vie also add a distinctive flavour to summer puddings and fruit compôtes.

Gin

Because of its dominant flavour, gin has to be used with more care than most other spirits. But it has its uses, especially for adding flavour to game dishes such as pheasant with red cabbage, or for flavouring marinades used to tenderise haunches of venison. Gin can also be used to complement the flavour of juniper berries in dishes such as sauerkraut and pork pâtés. The addition of gin to tomato soup works surprisingly well, too.

Pastis

Pastis is an exotic flavouring ingredient. It is used extensively in France to add flavour to dishes such as sea bass, rabbit and chicken, and to some regional dishes especially when they include fennel as an ingredient.

Rum

Rum is mostly used to flavour sweet dishes. It is especially effective when added to fried bananas, sweet omelettes, babas, rich fruit cakes and Christmas puddings.

Whisky

Whisky can add another flavour dimension to a variety of foods ranging from terrines to trifles. There is hardly a dish that it will not embellish when used judiciously, and if you run out of brandy, do not hesitate to use whisky in its place – and, of course, vice versa. Here are some suggestions of food dishes that can be enhanced by the inclusion of whisky as a flavouring ingredients:

- shellfish – prawns, lobster, scallops, shellfish soups, terrines, pâtés
- all meats, poultry, game
- chocolate marquise, chocolate mousse
- coffee sorbet, trifle
- fruit cakes and Christmas puddings.

Vodka

Vodka normally has no flavour, so it has very little to contribute to cookery. However, some Polish and Russian vodkas are flavoured with lemon, peppers, honey and so on; these will have more food-flavouring potential. A good example of flavoured vodka is *starka*, which is prepared from an infusion of Crimean apple leaves and pears with some brandy and port-style wine added. In Eastern Europe starka is sometimes used in marinades or to add flavour to fruit salads.

Liqueurs

As most liqueurs are sweet, they are in perfect harmony with dessert-course dishes. Fruit-based liqueurs are the most versatile, and flavour-winning partnerships include:

- kirsch with pineapple or cherries
- maraschino with fruit salads
- crême de cassis with blackcurrants
- crême de banane with bananas
- Grand Marnier ⎫
- orange curaçao ⎬ with orange soufflés and crêpes
- Cointreau ⎭
- crême de menthe in chocolate concoctions
- Baileys with puddings.

Almost any liqueur can be used with ice cream, but kahlúa or Cuarenta-y-Tres are recognised favourites. Try adding Bénédictine to cream fillings for trifles and sponge cakes.

The possibilities are endless. Just give rein to your imagination; with liqueurs experimentation is usually rewarded.

Recipes

The following recipes give further guidance as to the practical application of the use of spirits and liqueurs in cooking.

Whisky Terrine

(Serves 4)

Ingredients

250 g (8 oz) chicken livers
125 g (4 oz) streaky bacon
125 g (4 oz) button mushrooms
150 ml (5 fl oz) whisky
1 large onion, chopped
1 clove of garlic, crushed
grated rind and juice of 1 lemon
125 g (4 oz) butter
2½ tablespoons fresh white breadcrumbs
2 level tablespoons chopped fresh parsley
1 teaspoon thyme
salt and freshly ground black pepper
thyme, bay leaves and juniper berries or cranberries to garnish

Method

In a large pan melt the butter. Add the onion and garlic and cook on a low heat for 10 minutes. Remove the rind and chop the bacon, then add it together with chicken livers and mushrooms to the pan and cook for 5 minutes. Now add the whisky, lemon juice and the grated lemon rind. Mix and, after tasting, season as necessary. Cover the pan and allow the ingredients to simmer for 15 minutes. Stir occasionally. Remove from the heat, then place in a blender. Blend until smooth. Add the breadcrumbs, thyme and parsley and blend until smooth. Now put the terrine into a serving dish. Smooth the surface and decorate with thyme, bay leaves and juniper berries or cranberries. Cover with foil and chill in the fridge until required. Serve with thick, toasted bread.

Prawn Cocktail

(Serves 4)

Ingredients

340 g (12 oz) cooked and peeled prawns
4 tablespoons tomato sauce
4 tablespoons mayonnaise
2 teaspoons Worcestershire sauce
2 teaspoons lemon juice
3 tablespoons brandy
2 tablespoons thick or whipped cream
chopped parsley to garnish
1 small head of lettuce

Method

In a glass bowl mix together the tomato sauce, mayonnaise, Worcestershire sauce, lemon juice and brandy. Fold in the thick or whipped cream. Taste and adjust seasoning if necessary.

Into the bottom of each of four wine goblets put a couple of prawns and spoon a little of the sauce over them. Now add evenly alternate layers of finely shredded lettuce, prawns and sauce. Finish with a layer of prawns liberally covered with sauce. Decorate with finely chopped, fresh parsley. Buttered brown bread and a wedge of lemon are the accompaniments.

Crab Soup

(Serves 4–5)

Ingredients

150 g (6 oz) flaked crab
1 stick celery
1 chopped onion
1 potato, cut in cubes
1 bacon rasher, cut into small pieces
1 finely chopped clove of garlic
2 tablespoons double-concentrated tomato purée
1 tablespoon flour

1 tablespoon chopped parsley
1 litre (2 pints) fish stock
sunflower oil
bouquet garni
1 good measure brandy
salt and pepper
extra chopped parsley, butter and cream to garnish.

Method

Cover the base of a large saucepan with sunflower oil. Heat, then add the potato, bacon, finely chopped celery, onion and garlic. Sweat these ingredients in the hot oil. Add the tomato purée and reduce the heat, stirring continuously, and cook until vegetables are tender. Add the flour and cook for a further minute. Gradually, add the fish stock and bring to simmering point. Add the chopped parsley, bouquet garni and crab. Stir until heated through thoroughly. Add a good measure of brandy. Test for seasoning and correct if necessary. Heat until simmering then serve. Decorate with chopped, fresh parsley. This soup may also be finished with a knob of butter and a swirl of cream.

Salt Cod in a Creamy Calvados Sauce

(Serves 4)

Ingredients

1 kg (2¼ lb) salt cod
3 measures Calvados
300 ml (10 fl oz) cider
100 ml (3½ fl oz) crème fraîche
small bunch of fresh chervil
1 teaspoon English mustard
1 egg yolk
grated nutmeg
2 onions, 1 shallot
salt, pepper, bouquet garni

Method

Soak the cod in cold water for at least 24 hours – longer if the cod is very rigid. Then flake the cod and discard the skin and bones. Finely chop the onions, shallot and chervil. Halve the potatoes and place all these ingredients – including the fish – into a buttered casserole dish. Add seasoning and bouquet garni. Pour over the cider and two measures of Calvados. Add a knob of butter, cover tightly and cook on a low heat (160 °C/ 320 °F/ gas mark 2) for 50 minutes. When the potatoes are tender remove the bouquet garni. Take a tablespoon of the liquid from the casserole and put into a bowl together with the mustard, egg yolk, crème fraîche, a little nutmeg and the remaining Calvados. Beat well and add it to the casserole. Stir to blend. Leave to warm through for 5 minutes and serve on to hot plates.

Rabbit with Pastis

(Serves 6)

Ingredients

1 large rabbit prepared
3 measures pastis (Pernod or Ricard)
1 bunch fresh basil
a few fennel seeds
olive oil
strong mustard
salt and freshly ground black pepper

Method

Preheat oven to 170 °C/ 340 °F / gas mark 3.

Joint the rabbit into six portions. Smother each portion with strong-tasting mustard and place them in an ovenproof dish. Add a little olive oil. Sprinkle the fennel seeds and the finely chopped basil over the rabbit. Add salt and freshly ground black pepper. Cover with foil. Cook in the oven for 1 hour.

Before serving add the pastis and flame it. Be careful to stand well back. Serve with boiled or creamed potatoes or with rice.

Veal Escalopes with Prunes and Armagnac

(Serves 4)

Ingredients

4 x 90 g (3 oz) veal escalopes
300 ml (10 fl oz) chicken stock
125 ml (4 oz) of Armagnac
200 ml (7 fl oz) crème fraîche
20 pitted prunes
25 g (1 oz) butter
1 lemon

Method

Put the ready-to-eat, pitted prunes in a saucepan. Add the chicken stock and bring to the boil, then simmer, covered, for 5 minutes. Take 8 prunes out and keep them, covered, on a hot plate. These will be used later as part of the garnish. Boil the stock until it reduces by half. Purée the prunes together with the stock. Melt the butter in a pan, add the escalopes, season on both sides with salt and freshly ground black pepper. Cook for a couple of minutes each side. Add the Armagnac and flame the pan, taking care to stand well back from the flame. Remove the escalopes and keep them on a plate in the oven. Heat the purée of prunes and the crème fraîche in the pan. Season. Spoon a little on to each serving plate. Place the escalope on top, decorate each with the reserved prunes and a wedge of lemon. Serve with Lyonnaise potatoes (sauté potatoes with fried onions).

Beef Stroganoff

(Serves 1)

Ingredients

125 g (5 oz) fillet steak cut into strips 5 cm (2 inches) long and ½ cm (¼ inch) wide
50 g (2 oz) thinly sliced mushrooms
½ small chopped onion
60 ml (2 fl oz) sour cream
35 g (1½ oz) peeled, pickled gherkins

1 level teaspoon paprika
a little lemon juice
1 teaspoon French mustard
1 measure brandy

Method

Season the meat with salt and freshly ground pepper. Heat the butter in a pan over a high flame. Reduce the heat, add the paprika and cook for 2 minutes.

Add the steak, cook quickly until brown. Pour in the brandy and flame to burn off the fat. Remove the meat and keep hot in a covered hot plate. Reduce the heat, add the chopped onions and fry well in (extra) butter. Add the mushrooms and sliced gherkins, and stir in a teaspoon of French mustard. Blend well and add a few drops of lemon juice and sour cream. Taste and correct for seasoning. Add the meat to the sauce; the juice from the meat will reduce the sauce to the proper consistency. Heat the meat in the sauce, but do not boil as the meat will become tough. Blend the sauce with the meat. Serve on to a hot plate. Plain boiled potatoes or pilaff rice go well with this dish.

Steak Diane

(Serves 1)

Ingredients

1 fillet steak battered out to ½ cm (¼ inch) thickness
Worcestershire sauce
1 measure brandy
25 g (1 oz) finely chopped onion
25 g (1 oz) finely sliced mushrooms
25 g (1 oz) butter
finely chopped parsley
French mustard
single cream
salt, freshly ground black pepper

Method

Season the steak with salt and freshly ground black pepper on both sides. Put the butter in the pan and melt quickly.

Add the fillet steak and while it is cooking, massage some Worcestershire sauce into it with a fork. Turn the steak over and do exactly the same on the other side. Add one measure of brandy and flame. Without delay, remove the steak and keep it warm on a hot, covered plate.

Add the onion, and after a minute add the mushrooms. Cook until soft, then add some French mustard. Blend well. Remove the pan from the heat and add a little cream, blending all the ingredients well. Test for flavour. Adjust seasoning if necessary. Return the steak to the pan to heat through. Serve on a hot plate. Cover with the sauce and add a sprinkle of finely chopped parsley. Serve with fluffy mashed potatoes.

Banana Sublime

(Serves 2)

Ingredients

2 ripe bananas, skinned and halved lengthwise
1 teaspoon brown sugar
1 knob of butter
2 measures fresh orange juice
1 measure dark rum
1 measure crême de banane
2 scoops vanilla ice cream

Method

Heat the brown sugar in a pan over a medium flame, and wait for the sugar to begin to melt. Add the butter, melt and add the bananas. Fry quickly on both sides until the bananas are deep golden in appearance. Add the orange juice. Blend with the juices in the pan using the back of a fork.

Pour over the measure of rum.

Flame it and baste the bananas with the sauce.

Portion the bananas on to the two hot plates. Spoon over the sauce. Spoon the crême de banane liqueur over the bananas. Add the scoop of ice cream to each plate. Serve immediately.

Crêpes Suzette

(Serves 2)

Ingredients

4 thin pancakes (basic pancake mixture)
60 g (2 oz) caster sugar
60 g (2 oz) unsalted butter
1 measure Cointreau
1 measure Grand Marnier
1 measure brandy
2 lemons
2 large oranges
extra caster sugar in dredger

Method

Blend the butter and caster sugar together. Add a measure of
Cointreau and the very finely grated rind of one lemon and one
orange. Mix well, this is the basic sauce. Extract the juice from the
oranges and lemons.

Sprinkle the base of an omelette pan with caster sugar. Heat the pan,
and when the sugar begins to sweat and slightly darken, add most of
the basic sauce, but not all, as you may have to adjust later. Reduce
the heat, add most of the lemon juice and twice that amount of orange
juice – work in quickly with the back of a fork, otherwise you will get
a lumpy consistency which must be avoided. When the liquid is
smooth add the measure of Grand Marnier. Stir well, and taste; this
is the sauce that will be the major influence on the quality of the finished dish. At this stage the sauce should be rich but with a
discernible tartness. If it is too sweet balance the taste with a little
more lemon juice.

Now add the first pancake. Every pancake will have a good side – the
show side. Put the show side into the sauce. Baste with the sauce.
Sprinkle with caster sugar. Fold the pancake in half and then in half
again to form a fan shape. Move this to one corner of the pan. Add the
next pancake, repeat the procedure and place on top of the first pancake. Repeat with each pancake and stack.

Now put all the fan-shaped pancakes in to the sauce in the base of the
pan. Raise the heat and when the sauce is bubbling, sprinkle caster

sugar on to the edge of the pan that you are going to dip into the flame. Sugar has alcohol potential and you will get a more spectacular flame by doing this. Add the brandy into the area of the pan which you have sugared. Keep the pan level, count to five seconds until the spirit has gained the heat of the sauce. Dip the pan into the flame, and as it ignites use a spoon to flourish the flame all over the pan. Serve the crêpes on to two hot plates. Spoon the sauce over each pancake.

Tiramisu

(Serves 4)

Ingredients

250 g (8 oz) Mascarpone cheese
12–16 Savoiardi or Boudoir biscuits
2 measures kahlúa or dark rum
1 tablespoon caster sugar
1 tablespoon unsweetened cocoa powder
1 teaspoon vanilla essence
1 egg yolk
170 ml (6 fl oz) strong black coffee

Method

Put the egg, sugar, vanilla and 1 measure kahlúa or rum into a bowl and mix to a creamy consistency.

Add the Mascarpone and fold in to make a cream.

In another bowl stir together the coffee, which should be tepid, and the second measure of kahlúa or rum. Dip the biscuits, one by one, in the coffee mixture for a few seconds, letting each biscuit absorb enough liquid to keep firm, but not fall apart. Starting with the biscuits, arrange in four individual glass dishes alternate layers of biscuits and the Mascarpone cream ending with the Mascarpone.

Chill in the fridge for several hours to set. Serve straight from the fridge: it tastes better that way. Before serving, dust with the cocoa powder.

Irish Whiskey Trifle

(Serves 8–10)

Ingredients

1 large tin of fruit salad
2 Swiss rolls (without added cream)
2 bananas
5 measures Irish whiskey
1 packet of strawberry or raspberry jelly
600 ml (1 pint) custard (ready made or make your own)
sweetened whipped cream
cherries and almonds to decorate

Method

Line a large glass bowl with slices of one of the Swiss rolls. Sprinkle generously with Irish whiskey. Add the fruit salad and slices of the two bananas evenly; bananas give a wonderful flavour to any trifle. Melt the jelly using the syrup from the fruit salad, a little hot water and one measure Irish whiskey. Stir and pour half over the fruit. Cover with slices of the second Swiss roll. Again, sprinkle generously with Irish whiskey, and pour over the remaining jelly liquid.

When the jelly has set, top with the custard and decorate with cherries, almonds and peaks of sweetened whipped cream. Place in the refrigerator for 4 hours to settle before serving.

15

SOME QUESTIONS ANSWERED

Q Does drinking alcohol affect people more when they are airborne than when they are on dry land?

A Yes, alcohol affects people more when they are on an aeroplane. This is because the high cabin pressure forces the alcohol into the bloodstream more quickly. Additionally, the drier air in the cabin makes you feel more thirsty and consequently there is temptation to drink more to quench the thirst. Drinking alcohol also dehydrates the body which again makes you want to drink more. The effects of your alcohol consumption will be felt more on landing, so it is best to limit your consumption of alcohol when flying.

Q What is the best glass for drinking brandy?

A The type recommended by brandy distillers is the small balloon-shaped glass which is generally known as a snifter. The glass should be clear and fine enough to allow heat transference when hand held around the bowl. This stimulates the release of the delicate vapours known as the bouquet.

Q When not using a measure, how do you gauge how much brandy to pour without seeming to be too stingy or over-generous?

A Assuming you are using the small brandy balloon or snifter glass, a good rule is one-fifth brandy, four-fifths air. The air space allows the aromatic fragrances and the full, rich, harmonious aroma of the brandy to be savoured.

Another, but far more spectacular method of measuring is to pour an approximate measure into a snifter. Now place the glass on its side on a level table. If the measure is accurate it will fill the horizontal snifter to the point of overflowing, (see the front cover). And for your party trick, it should now be possible to roll the glass across the table to your partner without spilling a drop, provided of course that the table is absolutely level and smooth.

Q Some restaurants use special glass heaters to heat their brandy balloon glasses before serving brandy. Is this good practice?

A Not really, especially if the heaters are fuelled by methylated spirit. The fumes can permeate into the glass and ruin the bouquet of the brandy. Any excess heat will also destroy the bouquet.

Q What is the best way to store spirits?

A Whereas wine is stored horizontally to keep the cork moist and full in the bottle, spirits are best stored in an upright position, as prolonged contact with the cork will rot the cork and the spirits will take on that flavour. Spirits should be stored away from direct sunlight and strong odours. Extremes of temperature must also be avoided. A temperature of between 15 and 18°C (59–64°F) is ideal.

Q What is the best way to appreciate whisky?

A Gradually. You just don't rush in and buy the most expensive whisky and expect to be captivated by it. Perhaps the best way to start is by adding mixers – soda water, lemonade, ginger ale – to the less expensive blended whiskies. Then go onto enjoy a Whisky Mac (blended whisky and green ginger wine) which should really give you pleasant sensations. Then try de-luxe brands and see how you get on. Graduation to malt whiskies requires a good, experienced companion to give you sound advice. Start with the well-rounded, smooth and mellifluous malts. To cut down on expense, buy miniatures. Look at the colour and clarity, nose the whisky to appreciate the aroma. Take a sip and roll it around your mouth. Slowly swallow the whisky and let the sensations of taste work their way all over your mouth. Enjoy the after effects, the flowing lingering warmth in your mouth, the feeling of appreciation and goodwill in your mind. Now you can start trying the smoky peaty and full-blooded, grown-up tasting malts. Find out which one you really like. That's the one for you.

Q What is a Buyers Own Brand?

A Many distillers and blenders rely on supplying blends for resale under the Buyers Own Brand label. It is big business and is especially associated with supermarkets or, for example, a chain of restaurants. The suppliers of the spirit usually do not reveal the names of their customers. Very often the customers' cheaper brands are side by side on the shelves, along with the supplier's own more expensive brands.

Q If you are throwing a party, how many types of spirits and liqueurs do you need?

A People are very resilient. They will, very quickly, adjust to what is available. What you need is choice of three spirits and three liqueurs, and have plenty of mixers and ice available. Allow also for people who simply prefer beer or wine.

Q When serving liqueurs, what glass is best?

A The best glass of all is the small brandy balloon (snifter). This allows for the appreciation of the bouquet of the drink, as well as for additions such as crushed ice, cubed ice, cream, coffee beans and garnishes when required. The small elgin glass is cute but not very practical.

Q Can gin be drunk neat?

A Of course it can, but it has an overpowering flavour which the majority of people find off-putting, almost like tasting a nasty medicine. Gin needs a mixer, whether it be ice, water, Angostura bitters or – the favourite partnerships – tonic water or vermouth.

Q Is the quality and care of glassware important?

A Yes it is. We pay a lot of money for our spirits and liqueurs, so it is important to show them off to the best advantage. That means buying good-quality glassware of a shape and size appropriate to the drink being served. Glasses should feel good to handle and be clear and transparent, to ensure optimum visual impact which increases the pleasure of anticipation. They should also be odour free – in other words, brilliantly clean. To achieve this, glasses after washing should be rinsed in detergent-free hot water and dried and polished to a brilliance using clean, fresh glasscloths. They should be stored upright, so as not to trap stale air and preferably in a closed cupboard to keep dust at bay.

Q Why do spirits and liqueur prices vary so much?

A Some of the variation is caused by the quality of the different products. Quality can vary because of the ingredients used, the care and attention that went into the production, the length of maturation and the determined blending recipe. However, when comparing prices of a particular product you should be careful to compare capacity and the alcoholic strength by volume: they do vary! Proprietary brands also tend to command higher prices.

16
WEIGHTS AND MEASURES

Notes for American and Australian users

In America, the 8 fl oz measuring cup is used. In Australia, metric measures are used in conjunction with the standard 250 ml measuring cup. The Imperial pint, used in Britain and Australia, is 20 fl oz, while the American pint is 16 fl oz.

The British tablespoon holds 17.7 ml, the American 14.2 ml, and the Australian 20 ml. A teaspoon holds about 5 ml in all three countries.

British	American	Australian
1 teaspoon	1 teaspoon	1 teaspoon
1 tablespoon	1 tablespoon	1 tablespoon
2 tablespoons	3 tablespoons	2 tablespoons
3½ tablespoons	4 tablespoons	3 tablespoons
4 tablespoons	5 tablespoons	3½ tablespoons

An Imperial/American guide to measures

Solid measures

Imperial	American
1 lb butter	2 cups
1 lb flour	4 cups
1 lb sugar	2 cups
1 lb icing sugar	3 cups
8 oz rice	1 cup

Liquid measures

Imperial	American
¼ pint	⅔ cup
½ pint	1¼ cups
¾ pint	2 cups
1 pint	2½ cups
1½ pints	3¾ cups
2 pints	5 cups (2½ pints)

GLOSSARY

ABV alcohol by volume

ageing the maturing of some spirits in barrels usually made of oak. As the spirit rests in barrels air penetrates through the pores of the wood to mellow the distillate. Other wood substances such as tannin, lignin and vanilla will also have a bearing on the final character of the spirit. There is a correct time to stop the ageing process; prolonged ageing will impart an unfavourable woody flavour

aguardente Portuguese term for 'fire water' meaning grape brandy. In Spain, *aguardiente* also means grape brandy but when the term *de orujo* is added it means that the spirit was distilled from the pomace of crushed grapes.

alcohol the amount of potable ethyl alcohol (ethanol) C_2H_5OH found in a drink obtained by fermentation and further increased by distillation. Normally spirits are sold having an alcoholic strength of between 37.5 and 45 per cent. Liqueurs range from 17 to 55 per cent alcohol by volume

alembic a type of still used to produce styles of Cognac and Armagnac brandies in France

analyser the column in a continuous still in which the fermented wash is vaporised by steam

aqua vitae Latin for 'water of life'. This term was used in ancient times to describe spirits

bagaceira Portuguese brandy made from the pomace of crushed grapes

bitters spirits flavoured with aromatic fruits, herbs and plants; they all have a bitter taste, hence the name

blended whisky chiefly associated with Scotland where a number of malt whiskies are blended with grain whisky to formulate a particular brand. The aim of the blender is to produce a consistent taste that is associated with a named brand

BOB buyer's own brand: some spirits are made in a distillery for clients who want to market them under their own names

boisé essences of oak which are sometimes added to some brandies as they mature in cask. The addition of boisé enhances the tannin content and the aroma of oak. It also can impart an impression of maturity

bond after distillation spirits are kept in bonded warehouses under government supervision. Duty is not paid while the spirits mature in the warehouses. Once the spirits are required for sale, excise duty must then be paid before the spirits are released for sale

bonne chauffe 'the good heating' or second distillation in the making of Cognac. The first distillation is known as *brouillis* ('boiling up')

botanicals the flavourings added to neutral spirit to produce gin

cask a barrel, usually made of oak, for maturing spirits; sizes vary

chaser usually a glass of beer (or water) that chases down a glass of spirit. Some people reverse the order, but the idea of the spirit first is to warm the stomach in preparation for the cold beer to follow

compound a mixture of several ingredients used to flavour spirits such as gin and sundry liqueurs

condenser an apparatus which liquefies the alcoholic vapours as they emerge from a still

congeners flavour and aroma elements which organic compounds impart to fermented and distilled drinks. The higher the strength of distillation, the fewer the congeners

cooler a long drink with a spirit base, topped up with fruit juice such as lemon or lime juice. Ice, and sometimes soda water, is added

cordial a drink that stimulates the heart (*Cor Cordis* – heart). Associated with sweetened and flavoured spirits – liqueurs

decanter a stoppered, glass container used to display wines, spirits and liqueurs. They come in various shapes. Some are highly ornamented and some liqueur decanters are quite spectacular being multi-columned with each compartment designed to hold an individual and differently coloured liqueur

distilling the boiling of a fermented liquid, capturing and condensing the vapours into a new liquid which will have a much higher alcoholic strength

dram a measure of Scottish whisky

eau de vie French term for a spirit: *eau de vie de vin* is brandy; *eau de vie de cidre* is Calvados

esters the combination of acids and alcohol which form the volatile substance that gives spirits and other alcoholic drinks their aroma

fermentation the action of yeast enzymes on sugar which convert the sugar into alcohol and carbon dioxide

fine a good-quality brandy produced in France. *Fine maison* is the house brandy offering good value in bars or restaurants. *Fine champagne* is a superb style of Cognac brandy

firewater native American name for whiskey

foreshots and feints the first and last part of the distillation of Scotch whisky, known also as heads and tails. They contain unpleasant by-products and are held aside and later sent back for redistilling

frappé associated with some liqueurs which are poured into a glass which contains crushed ice

fusel oil toxic alcohol – not ethanol – found in spirits as a by-product of distillation. Discarded with the removal of the heads and tails

garnish a decoration added to give a drink 'eye appeal'

grain whisky a light, blending whisky made in Scotland from maize (corn) using the continuous-still method of distillation

grape brandy brandy distilled from wine as distinct from a brandy such as marc or grappa which is usually distilled from the pomace or debris left over after the grape pressing

grist coarse-ground malted barley used in the production of beer and in the distillation of whisky. It is mashed or mixed with hot water to extract the sugars required for fermentation

heart the centre or best part of a distillation run produced by the pot-still method. Also known as the middle cut, it is the fraction that is put into cask to be matured

hydrometer the instrument that determines and records the density or specific gravity of alcohol in a liquid

infusion the steeping or soaking of flavouring materials in alcohol so that the flavours will permeate the spirit

jersey lightning an American term for applejack brandy. Not to be confused with the apple brandy made in Jersey in the Channel Islands

kiln a furnace or drying oven which is used to halt further germination of the barley on its way to becoming malt. The original heat source was peat but now other fuels are also used. Malt is, of course, a prime ingredient in the production of malt whisky

lees the debris left behind after the fermentation of wine. Consists of yeasts, grape skins and some solid matter. Lees are used in the making of pomace brandy

limousin a forest near Limoges in France famous for the distinctive quality of its oak trees. The wood from the trees, when matured, is made into casks in which the great Cognac brandies and some other spirits are matured. The wood is excellent for maturation and it also imparts some colour and flavour elements to a spirit

low wines the product of the first distillation in the wash still, during the making of Scotch whisky

malt barley that has been steeped, germinated and kiln dried in order to convert the starch within the grain into fermentable sugars. The malt is then ground into grist and mashed with hot water to extract the sugars

malt whisky whisky made entirely from malted barley

marc a French pomace brandy made in most wine regions in France. Best known are Marc de Bourgogne and Marc de Champagne

marrying the process of allowing distillates which have been recently blended to settle and harmonise

mash the combination of malted barley grist and hot water. This is mixed and agitated in a mash tun to extract the sugars. The liquid is then known as wort

moonshine illegally distilled American whiskey particularly sought after during the years of Prohibition 1920–33. Sometimes called Mountain Dew

Napoléon name seen often on brandy labels and meant to imply quality and maturity

neat a spirit that is drunk undiluted

Nelson's blood Royal Navy term for rum

nosing the professional way of determining the merits of spirits. Spirit blenders work entirely by nose. The spirits are sniffed gently. Sometimes a little water is added to help the spirit to reveal its true aromas. Water creates a chemical reaction, releasing heat to unfold the complete array of fragrances

oak weathered oak casks are generally acknowledged to be the very best for maturing wines, spirits and, when necessary, liqueurs. The finest-quality oak is believed to come from the forests of Limousin and Tronçais in France and from America. The porosity of oak allows a slow oxidation critical to the development of mellowness and finesse. Spirits especially, by their interaction with oak, extract tannin, colour and flavour from the wood. But new oak casks are used sparingly as they are very absorbent and can overwhelm a drink with an unattractive woodiness. Spirits only improve while maturing in wooden casks; once bottled they remain constant

pagoda head attractive, pyramid chimneys that are traditionally placed above the kilns in Scottish distilleries. They have become a feature of the Scottish landscape and indicate where distilleries are located

peat reek the peat smoke that permeates malted barley in the production of some whiskies. The degree of peatiness can be controlled. Whiskies influenced by peat reek will have a light, medium or heavy smoky flavour

Phylloxera vastatrix aphid or vine louse which feeds on the roots of vines and kills them. It devastated most world vineyards in the late 1800s and consequently affected the production of Cognac and many other brandies. The louse cannot be eradicated, but it can be controlled by grafting the classic European *Vitis vinifera* scion on to native American root stocks which are immune to the vine pest

pomace the residue left behind after the extraction of the juice from grapes and other fruit

poteen illicit whiskey distilled in Ireland. Also called Mountain Dew

pot still the classic still in which all the highly flavoured spirits such as malt whisky, brandy and dark rums are made

Prohibition the United States' attempt to outlaw the production for sale of all alcoholic drinks. Prohibition started one minute after midnight on 17 January 1920; it ended at 5:30 p.m. on 23 December 1933. It became known as the Volstead Act, named after Andrew Volstead the 'dry' representative for Minnesota who was instrumental in getting the 18th Amendment past the various stages. He had the backing of the powerful temperance movement and the uncompromising religious leaders and others who felt that alcohol undermined the structure of family life. All Prohibition achieved was to put legitimate distillers out of business and let loose unscrupulous bootleggers and smugglers who prospered in selling the most terrible concoctions including bathtub gin and white mule (rough whisky) to a thirsty public

proof most countries now express the strength of a liquid in terms of the percentage of alcohol by volume. The United States still uses the proof system of measurement which determines pure alcohol to be 200° proof. Each degree proof equals one-half per cent of alcohol. So a US spirit being sold at 80° proof would contain 40 per cent alcohol by volume

rancio associated with the taste of aroma of aged brandy that has peaked but is still a delight to drink

rectification the purifying of a spirit by redistillation

rectifier the second column in the continuous or patent still, in which the alcoholic vapours received from the analyser are condensed

red eye American term for raw, firey whiskey. Sometimes called rotgut

rocks a drink 'on the rocks' will be undiluted and served with ice cubes

Saladin box the box or trough where barley is turned by chain-driven turners in the malting process. The system was invented by M. Saladin, a Frenchman

self whisky a single malt whisky that is usually destined to be sold as a stand-alone whisky rather than being used for blending purposes

serpantin a spiral-shaped, copper pipe used in France to hold the alcoholic vapours as they emerge from the pot still. The pipe is submerged in a tank of cold water and the vapours are condensed

silent spirit a completely neutral spirit of high strength but without flavour and aroma

single malt a malt whisky produced uniquely in one single distillery

slainte pronounced *slauncha* is a Gaelic drinking expression meaning 'good health'

sour mash the residue from a previous fermentation which is added to the new mash in the production of some bourbon whiskies

spirit safe a control box usually made of glass and brass and used by distillers to separate the different fractions – heads, hearts and tails – of a distillate

stills the vessels in which fermented liquids are distilled. The two principal stills used are the pot still and the continuous or patent still which is also known as the Coffey still after the man who patented it

straight whiskey a term used in the United States to indicate that the whiskey has not been blended with neutral spirit before being bottled; if it had it would be sold as blended whiskey

Tronçais one of the great oak forests in France. Its wood is highly prized for maturing wines, brandies and eaux de vie

uisge beatha the Gaelic term for 'water of life'; the first word inspired the English to call the spirit whisky

vatted malt a group of single malts from different distilleries, and very likely from the same region in Scotland, are mixed and married together in a vat to make a particular brand. Sometimes called 'pure malts' for that is what they are

warehouse a huge building in which casks of whisky rest and mature. The floors may be of earth which absorbs moisture during damp weather and which beneficially moisturises the atmosphere in hot weather

wash a fermented alcoholic liquid which is intended for distillation

Weinbrand grape brandy usually of German origin. When the word *uralt*, as in Asbach Uralt, is used it means the producing distillery is very old or ancient

Whiskey Mick a combination of Irish whiskey and ginger wine

Whisky Mac a combination of Scotch whisky and ginger wine

Whisky Toddy taken to fight a cold or as a nightcap; a comforting mixture of whisky, sugar, lemon juice and hot water

worm associated with the pot still, it is a coil of copper tubing which holds the alcoholic vapours during condensation

wort the sugary liquid obtained by mashing malted barley and hot water in the mash tun. When cooled the wort will be fermented into distillers' beer

yeast general term for the single-celled microorganisms that produce zymase, which is the enzyme that converts sugar into alcohol

FURTHER READING

Brown, G. *Classic Spirits of the World*, London: Multimedia Books Limited, 1995.

Darton, M. (ed.) *Cocktails*, London: Quintet Publishing Ltd, 1990.

Doxat, J. *Drinks and Drinking*, London: Ward Lock, 1971.

Dunkling, L. *The Guinness Drinking Companion*, London: Guinness Publishing, 1992.

Durkan, A. *Vendange*, London: Edward Arnold, 1971.

Durkan, A. and Cousins, J. *The Beverage Book*, London: Hodder & Stoughton, 1995.

Fielden, C. *Exploring Wines and Spirits*, London: Wine and Spirit Education Trust, 1994.

Grossman, H.J. *Grossman's Guide to Wines, Spirits and Beers*, New York: Charles and Scribner's Sons, 1964.

Hallgarten, P. *Spirits and Liqueurs*, London: Faber & Faber Ltd, 1983

Lichine, A. *Encyclopaedia of Wines and Spirits*, London: Cassell, 1967.

McCreary, A. *Spirit of the Age, The Story of "Old Bushmills"*, Belfast: The Universities Press (Belfast) Ltd, 1983.

McNulty, H. *Liqueurs and Spirits*, London: Octopus Books, 1985.

Milroy, W. *Malt Whisky Almanac*, Moffat, Scotland: Lochar Publishing, 1989.

Opperman, D.J. (ed.) *Spirit of the Vine*, Cape Town, South Africa: Human & Rousseau Publishers (PTY) Ltd, 1968.

The Savoy Cocktail Book (reprinted 1989), London: Constable.

Shaw, C.P. *Collins Gem Whisky*, Glasgow: HarperCollins, 1995.

Waugh, A. *Wines and Spirits*, New York: Time–Life Books, 1968.

INDEX